# The Human Upgrade

## The Power to Create Your Future

Naomi Sesay

authorHOUSE®

*AuthorHouse™ UK Ltd.*
*500 Avebury Boulevard*
*Central Milton Keynes, MK9 2BE*
*www.authorhouse.co.uk*

*Phone: 08001974150*

*First published by AuthorHouse  4/9/2009*

*ISBN: 978-1-4389-4749-5 (sc)*

*Printed in the United States of America*
*Bloomington, Indiana*

*This book is printed on acid-free paper.*

For
Dante, Cidhalia and Dario
Always with love

# Contents

# Acknowledgements

I think everybody has a book that is waiting to come out and shine to the world. Words are powerful and they create a tremendous amount of change, especially if they are truly felt by the writer. However, no writer is complete without their barrage of experts, friends, families and loving eagle-eyed critiques. My first thanks goes to my wonderful, powerful, elegant mother, Martha Sesay who showed me the way to self mastery. The proof of the pudding is definitely in the eating. Everyone always asks where do I find the time to do all what I do AND raise three children? The answer lies within the beauty, patience and understanding of those three insightful leaders of the next generation – I am proud of you all. Anna and Adama, you travelled the road with me, and you both continue to do so. I am honoured to be walking beside such phenomenal women –P3. A big thank you to you

Leda, you kept me sane. Thanks to Harun, Francine, Geoffrey and Richard, my SOCHA School dream team. I would like to thank all the BLC ladies for their unwitting support and unconditional love, especially Heather – who thoroughly polished the manuscript. To Gennaro Draisci, thanks for designing the front cover and finally, I extend my gratitude to Antonio, (more than you'll ever know), and to those of you who bought this book.

# Before

Can you imagine that my best friend called me a witch – in this day age? Okay, we were just at the end of the 20th century but can you believe it? She called me a witch! And yes she meant it; I could see it in her eyes. I suspected something was going on a long time ago; in fact it all started happening when I was around twelve years of age...

## Many Years Ago...

I simply asked my younger sister to get me the red apple from the kitchen as she was on her way there. On returning, she was just about to hand me the apple when my mother, who was lying on the sofa took it from her and said, "Thank you".

I stared incredulously at my mother.

"That apple was meant for me," I told her as RESPECTFULLY as I could muster.
"Go and get another one," she said flippantly.

I swallowed and began to get hot, as I felt an argument about to brew. "There isn't another red apple mum, that's the last one and that's why I asked for it," I said, as evenly as I could. She just looked at me and coolly proceeded to take a bite.

Take a bite?! She was about to take a FREAKING bite!!!!

Red was the only colour I could see and it wasn't just the apple. I was so flabbergasted that I stared at her with my mouth wide opened in horror, willing the apple to fly out of her hands.

All of a sudden the apple literally fell out of her hands and rolled towards me. How flipping rude, I thought. I figured that my mother insolently tossed the apple at me because I was making such a fuss. As it turned out she declared that the apple was pulled away from her by my negative energy and that I could take the apple because she had lost her appetite for it!!! What? What!! I thought, what on earth is she saying? My mind was racing trying to keep up with her crazy speech again, which wasn't always easy.

She said that the apple was literally pulled out of her hands and rolled towards me because of the force of my energy and because I intended it to be so and in that respect, she didn't want the apple any more. It was mine. "Nonsense," I retorted, silently under my breath. She just didn't want to admit that the apple just accidentally fell out of her hands and rolled over to me so she considered it unworthy. My mother looked at me thoughtfully, coolly even, and didn't even try to convince me of her theory. Her irritating look of 'knowing' suddenly unnerved me and made me feel curious at the same time. As hot and irritated as I was, I decided to ignore the incident. So I picked up the apple, dusted it off and savagely bit in to it!

A few months later another incident occurred. Do you remember back in the days when you really loved a television program and after school you would run home just to catch the next episode? Well my favourite programme at the time was *Grange Hill* and I rushed home to watch the last episode. Just as I was settling in to the sofa after tossing my books on the coffee table, which accidentally slid to the floor, I heard my mother calling my name. I inwardly groaned and sank deeper in to my comfortable seat hoping she would forget to call out my name for the next thirty minutes or so. I was wrong, "Naomi!" she shrilled, "go and tidy your room right now; it's a disgrace."
"I will after *Grange Hill*, Mum."
"No, now,"
"Pleeaaaasssse," I implored, "after I have fini…"
"You better get yourself up those stairs young lady or you and I will wear the same trousers."

That was her way of saying that I was going to regret setting eyes on the TV if I didn't do what she asked me to do that second.

Boy was I fuming. I was experiencing that frustrated anger, knowing you have no control in your mother's house, that made me want to blow my top. Deathly angry, I grabbed the vacuum cleaner, stormed upstairs to my room, dumped the cleaner on the floor and sat heavily on my bed. I was so mad I couldn't even cry. Just then, something weird happened. The light bulb suddenly smashed and pieces of glass fell down onto the burgundy carpeted floor. I was stunned. I looked up to see no glass around the fused wire that was once a light bulb. I kept looking up and down wondering what the hell happened just now.

Suddenly I had a feeling that my mum was going to blame me for this and I ran downstairs to tell her the truth of what happened, desperately hoping to divert an all out war and to perhaps gain a little sympathy for myself. You know what she said? With one hand on her hips and the other hand wagging a finger in my face that nearly poked my eye out, she said, "That was your bad energy, now go back up stairs and clean it, and do it properly. And you better check yourself young lady before you get yourself in to some fine trouble". Again I was stunned in to silence. What was she saying? She was blaming me after all, well not me, my energy! I was so dazed and confused that *Grange Hill* suddenly dimmed into the background.

## Beings of ultimate power

So, what is it? What was creating all of these phenomena? Over the years and many incidences later, I knew without a shadow of doubt that I was tapping in to something so powerful and intrinsic embedded in all of us human beings that I became a ferocious researcher to find the tangible answer. We are Beings of Ultimate Power and my search to prove it has led me to documenting these very (non) secrets right here in the book you are now holding.

## We are magical creatures

So, what makes human beings so special? What is the essence that allows for every human being to sparkle more brightly than the stars and excel themselves in the most breathtaking ways? Take Oprah Winfrey for example – how was it possible that an abused young black girl rose up from her poor, angst ridden background to become the richest black woman in the media world? A billionaire none the less? What successful (and secret) path did she discover and how was it that she was able to locate that path? What made her super aware of the winds of change she was destined to create? Or was she consciously aware of it at all? And if she wasn't, what inexplicable force pulled her to create the phenomenal woman she is today? I wanted to know.

Another example – Bill Gates. What fate of 'luck' put him in the right position at the right time to seize the right opportunity that made him into the richest man on the globe and then to give up all his wealth to create a greater global cause? Yes, I definitely wanted to know because I felt something unusual was happening to me and it was unravelling itself on a very conscious level.

# Living in Phenomena

Phenomena are strange things. Billions of people experience miracle phenomena in their lives and yet they ignore them, preferring to live in the safe and banal ordinary world knowing that there was something 'bizarre' about 'that particular experience'. However, our vernacular of description fails to articulate or capture that esoteric fleeting moment. As a consequence, we negate these fascinating experiences and throw them in to the 'freaky bin', only for the anomalies to come out again at parties where they compare with others who experience miraculous phenomena. We then laugh at the weirdness of it all. Haven't you noticed this? Haven't you noticed that when you laughed at those certain incidences you also produced a freaky, excited 'high' sensation in your emotions, which excited and prompted you to talk even more about weird stuff? Or perhaps you are one of those people who are so freaked out about the whole thing that you pass it off as pure nonsense or a quirk of nature. Are you not curious to find out how and why these experiences are occurring?

I am not going to pull any punches in this book and I will not entice you with dazzling personal development type words that are not relevant to the text with the purpose of confusing your senses. Looking at the state of the world we live in right now we haven't got much time for fruitless intellectual activities. We need foresight and we need action. Most of all we need some serious attitude changes in our societies. It starts with only one person and you know who that person is, right? Yep, you guessed it: you.

So, please, if at anytime you do not resonate with any of what you are about to read, then DO NOT dismiss it!! Be an explorer, a pioneer or even just plain old curious and investigate it. Go and have a debate about it, talk about it, shift it around and scream and shout about it until you are so exhausted that you start to feel what I am saying. One thing I know for sure in this life is this: if we do not do something different to what we have always done then we are doomed to get the same results as we have always gotten. Look around you, your environment, your lifestyle, your job, the state of the world. Would you like to keep any of it the same forever and ever, without change? Or are you willing to walk the paths of the glorious unknown? For I am about to give you my version of how things may be; another insightful contribution to the ocean of rising awareness in which we are all entangled.

Are you ready? Come let's explore…

Oh and by the way, before we get started, I make no apologies for all the questions I am going to ask at the beginning of this book. They are designed to prod your imagination! Remember, do and think something different and you will experience a different result.

# Chapter One – The Essence of Life

Let's examine the contents of our freaky box! Have you ever experienced a 'coincidence' that made you exclaim the word "WOW?" Did you ever wonder how those coincidences came about? And have you not realised yet that these miraculous phenomena were actually created by YOU and you will keep on doing it unconsciously until you wake up and start doing it consciously?

The fact is you are truly in complete control of your own reality. That is, you create every circumstance, emotion, event and outcome that you experience. I can feel some of you balking at this sentence already. Perhaps you are remembering an injustice done against you and you are now declaring a complete denial of responsibility. That's natural, so just hang on in there for a while. The truth is, most of the time we create our experience on auto pilot using the unconscious conditionings that we were brought up with. The information needed to understand this truth has hardly been revealed to any of us due to the current levels of our education. Our education system is at best stifling and at worst, non productive. Our conditioning creates distortions of our reality so we create our journeys according to how we have been conditioned. So it feels like everything around and outside of us is happening TO us and we have little or no control over the events that create our destinies. For example, have you ever been told that you were exactly like one of your parents when you vowed you would never be? Or you do the same things over and over again without realising that there is a pattern until the pattern rears its ugly head... yet again? What is it that makes us repeat ourselves, even though we swore blind that we would never choose that certain type of someone again?

It all lies within our programming. We have been programmed from the moment we existed to develop a certain pattern or learning curve that carves out our experiences. That cloth was cut for us by our parents societies, environments and institutions. In most cases it was not done deliberately or even consciously, it is just that we humans are so remarkable that we have the ability to absorb and download billions of bits of information in a very short period of time – and aptly learn and apply it. Therefore learnt actions, behaviours, tones, emotional responses are all logged in to our systems before we even reach the age of six years. We thus put ourselves in a very un-resourceful and disadvantageous position in life. Imagine this: we come into this world equipped with all the natural hardware (our brains and bodies) we need to download and run the beautiful software (information gained from a highly intelligent source) of our lives that we are hoping to install. We are also hoping that some responsible adult that physically created us will give us the best chance we can get, given our chosen circumstances. However, what we didn't realise is that most of us are given a corrupt software system that we run over and over again until it feels like the system is actually part of our hardware and we were just 'born like that'! The worst part is that we don't even realise that we can upgrade our software at any time.

For those of us who haven't heard of this notion before, it's time to wake up and join the journey. If you have heard of this concept before then great, we are about to go even deeper.

So here is the question: how are we creating our reality, specifically?

## Intricate Layers of Information

Let's take this one step at a time.

Have you ever wondered what powers you? What makes you do the things that you would not normally do, especially if you are faced with serious threat to your survival? What gives you the strength to carry on when every ounce of your psyche screams, "No more, enough is enough". What makes your whole body function from the day you were conceived, pumping blood around your body, creating biochemical cocktails, giving you sensory information, all without your initial conscious knowledge, and still it will not give up until the day you die?

In July 2008, a five year old girl and her father were travelling down a country road when the father lost control of the car. He said he last remembered seeing grass through the windscreen and then nothing. Two days later, he woke up and found himself in hospital with five broken ribs a ruptured spleen and a daughter to thank. What happened?

Well, that five year old girl needed her father to be alive. Still strapped in the car and seeing her father hanging out of it, lifeless, she had not known that he had internal bleeding and was near to death. The girl suffered a broken bone near her eye, was bleeding, crying and was scared.

But she was determined to do one thing, and that was to keep her father alive. So she set out on the road to look for help, and when she found a man cutting the grass on his lawn, she was able to direct him a mile down the road to her grandmother's house. Help came immediately and the father and child are alive and well. What drove that girl in the midst of panic and shock to calmly walk down the road and direct strangers to her grandmother's house a mile away? What information did she posses that would not allow this horrific situation to continue its supposedly natural course?

Most of us are aware of people curing themselves of cancer and surviving horrific accidents that should have been fatal or even going through a Near Death Experience, which is a phenomenon that the medical field are still baffled about. These things are only possible through the remarkable source or field which I consider the essence of life. It is the extraordinary binding agent that some call the zero point field, ether, the matrix and so on. This source is highly intelligent, highly malleable and completely non judgmental. It is the hub of being and each and every one of us is wholly and unequivocally created from this source. We are, in essence, the manifestation of this source's consciousness.

Think about it. Every day, we see people chronically abusing their bodies with drugs, alcohol, food and habitual negative thoughts and emotional processes, deadly fumes and other poisons, but that body still gets up in the morning and still functions – still strives to become healthy and live another day until eventually we annihilate that body through our lifestyles! But the information of our bodies has evolved and adapted itself so remarkably well that if someone who lived even one hundred years ago suddenly turned up here in the 21st century, they would certainly find it a challenge to stay alive. If the disease that we are all mostly immune to didn't get them then the noise and confusing technology certainly would!

It is as though the body has a certain purpose and will not give up until the exact moment it chooses to expire. Could the body have a life agenda all on its own, independent of what you conditionally think? After all, what is a reflex if not the body acting on a stimulus before you even have a conscious inkling of what caused that stimulus? Pretend to throw a ball at someone's face and watch them blink before they even realised what happened. That reflex comes from a highly intelligent and protective source. If that is the case then who is running your body independently from the conscious you? You, your body, your subconscious mind or another player? Hmmm – what's going on here?

It is fascinating how human beings are able to commit acts of heroism in moments of pure desperation or duress without even thinking about it. Most of us have probably heard of the desperate mother who effortlessly picked up a car to release her trapped child. If she was asked to pick up that same car whilst she was in an ordinary state of consciousness, she would not have been able to. At that moment, there was something very definite and extraordinary that instantly created a decision and a do or die attitude that propelled this mother into an unthinking state of action. This definitely spells out that most of the time our thinking is an inferior conscious state of mind compared to the highly intelligent and intuitive state of being.

Reduction scientists may argue that the automatic action came from a reflex response that was programmed in our subconscious mind. That is absolutely true, but who supplied the 'software' for that information to be programmed in the first place and when precisely was that particular bit of information programmed in when obviously it was a future event that had not been foreseen yet? Or had it? More on this later.

# Light Beings

It is agreed in science that we are made up of tiny little photons of light. If we were to strip away the cells and their membranes, get rid of the molecules with the compounds and sugars, and get down to the nucleus, we could magnify the atom. Clever scientists have known for a long time that what is around the atom are sub-atomic particles like the electron zipping around the nucleus of the atom playing strange cohesive games. Now you see them, now you don't – we can't even see if they are really there! On closer inspection the photons seem to be fuzzy stuff that resembles and sometimes behaves just like pure energy – clouds of it that can and do appear whenever and however they like – it depends on who is observing the curious activities or maybe I should say festivities because this is where it starts to get fun.

However, let's back up a little. If the very core of our cells are only, and I don't say 'only' too lightly, made up of energy, then we, as a whole are just made up of energy. Light Energy. Now, please take my hand and follow me. If we are just made up of energy which is very, very light indeed - that is high vibratory frequency- then we are not solid mass as some of us believe we are. That is a perception of our dense five senses. We are in fact floating beings of light!

In our reality we feel and look solid and heavy but that is only because our senses (the five that we are aware of that we regularly use) vibrate at a lower frequency. Lower than that of light. So like a movie that has been slowed down, we perceive things in chunks of low light. Like chunks of old silent movies when the projector ran out of power and s l o w e d    d o w n. The light that is us is imbued with a trillion bits of information. This information forms and coherently configures itself into different frequencies and matrices, which give the sense of shade and light, form and matter. The amount of information that is held in all types of energy is mind boggling to the conscious human mind. However, all of the information that is available to decode this energetic information is stored in our subconscious mind waiting to be tapped and utilised. This information is accurately and miraculously organised and accurately deciphered by US (Universal Souls, you and me in other words) in the most profound and simplest of ways. At this present time in humanity, we are taking more and more of this information and bringing it into our conscious minds and deciphering it in phenomenal ways. We feel confused or feel like we are searching for something because we are processing new information that has not been felt consciously before.   It is not a surprise that there are thousands of new workshops to choose from, all geared to process and make sense of our new reality.

On a physical level our brains translate these chunks of light into information that we can relate to in order to conduct our lives on earth. These bits of information are in forms of pictures, words, feelings, smells, etc. Earth has a unique frequency which is slowed down even further because of the mysterious and wonderful energy force we call gravity. We are living in force fields of different polarities every moment we exist. These polarities play a huge part in the way we feel about things. More on this later. We know a great deal about gravity; it is now time to go to the other end of the spectrum and learn about the high frequency fields we swim in. Are your ready?

## The Power of Energy

Energy cannot be contained, created or destroyed. It just is. It can be directed, expanded, manipulated, compressed and all sorts of other fantastic things, which is why we are able to create the things we create on this earth. The different organs in our bodies all posses different energy frequencies configured in different ways. Therefore they hold different information and of course that is why different organs look different - because their energy information is different!

When we compare two heart organs from two different human beings, they hold the same type of heart frequency which gives the information for creating the heart structure but they may hold slightly different energy configurations which makes each person unique.

Therefore, each cell in our bodies holds and reproduces its own unique energy information. It gains its information from the pool of information that is within our bio energy field or the subconscious mind, and at any one time our bio energy field is dynamically changing due to our thoughts and our environment. Our DNA, as it is also an energy field, adapts itself according to the information that it is fed within this field. As all this information collides and colludes with each other, it creates a beautiful medley of form operating on a specific vibratory frequency. This form is called the human body. As energy is dynamic and unbounded, it radiates off the physical body (photon emissions) creating another form of body which is not as dense. Sometimes we perceive this as just heat emanating from another persons skin but what is heat if not energy and if energy contains billions of bits of information, how much information can you read off someone else's body heat? How sexy is that?

I am sure you have experienced walking into a room and knowing without even hearing a word that something terrible or unpleasant has just happened. One could cut the atmosphere with a knife, we like to say. Or perhaps you were walking down a familiar road late one evening and suddenly you stopped dead in your tracks and felt that you wanted to go another way even though it would take you much longer and even though you haven't seen anything that has alerted you to danger. How come you suddenly felt this feeling? It is because your higher intelligence read the information before your conscious mind did. It then transformed the information into an emotion and you gave that emotion meaning then acted accordingly to your reality. Your programmed conditioning further sautés this information by dissecting and analysing the meaning then making you act according to your way of looking at your own reality.

Sometimes we walk past people and are instantly energetically repelled without even knowing why and sometimes we feel so magnetised to someone we just met that we literally feel we have fallen in love. Our energy fields are constantly pulsating in and out with resonance as we interact with the environment around us – how incredibly sexy is that? This constant energy resonance is the crux of our power because it gives us clues to how we conduct ourselves within our environment, particularly when it is infused with an unshakable conviction of emotions emanating from our self belief.

As the energy information from the body radiates out, it becomes less dense and forms a just about visible energy field around your physical body. It doesn't stop there. Your field radiates out to touch infinite amounts of objects that make up our universe; therefore, you are literally connected to everything in the universe. When you exude a powerful magnetic resonance, just imagine what happens – yep, the world is in the palm of your hands. Treat it gently and respectfully and you will unleash the secrets of powerful creation.

Just think of your body as an ice cube. The ice cube is solid, hard and dense as the $H_2O$ vibrates at a lower frequency. The electrons and therefore energy information are dense and compacted. They are slow moving. What happens when you heat up the ice with a Bunsen burner? Like the good old Cointreau ad, the ice melts. (Go back 25 years and you may catch the commercial on TV!) The vibratory frequencies of the electrons have risen and that means the newly formed liquid is free to move lusciously and elegantly. Remember, it is still $H_2O$, the same chemical property as the ice. So, what happens when you heat up the liquid? Yep, that's right. The vibratory frequency rises yet again and steam starts to form. It's lighter and almost invisible but you know it is there. It still carries the same information, $H_2O$. And then what happens when you heat up steam? It is very easy now to understand that there is higher vibratory energy forms that we cannot see but still exist, right?

Our bodies emanate the same pattern and process of information at higher and higher frequencies. However, because we are complex creatures, we also carry a lot of our informational baggage with us in our bio energy systems which we happily, unwittingly and noxiously create with our intentions, emotions, thoughts and mental activities.

Let's think about this – if our energy fields emanate from our bodies constantly as they cannot be contained, then we are intimately and continually entwined and entangled with one another and indeed with everything else, as it is all energy. This means that on a higher level and in terms of combining our individual energetic information, we are truly... ONE. One energy field, one substance, one creation, one thought, one purpose. However, because we are configured in slightly different ways we are individuated in to trillions of different forms. We did that - by virtue of our collective consciousness! How we did that is another book called *Soul Games*. So what's stopping us from leveraging from our vast informational field, and thus creating our own individual destinies? It is the act of not knowing. The key is in the way we run our informational energy system through our emotional thought and mental activities together, with the knowledge of how to do this.

A couple of months ago, I was invited to a large workshop of delegates who were interested in learning how to be effective life coaches. I felt a little out of place as I had gone through these processes years ago, yet I understood that it was possible for me to pick up contacts and friends that may come in useful for later relations. I walked into that room with the sole purpose of making the most contact and saying the least words. During an exercise on rapport, the facilitator asked everyone who they thought created the most rapport in the room. To my surprise, many people pointed at me. I was surprised because it was only 11.30 in the morning and I had hardly spoken. I was asked to stand up and the delegates were quizzed as to why they felt I had created the most rapport in the room. Lovely words of praise were expressed concerning my smile, the act of listening, being present, etc. The real reason was because I came into that room that morning with the state of KNOWING that I had already established contacts and friends and my resonant energy field relayed that message the moment I FELT that truth. As soon as I felt that truth, everyone else sensed it too. Do you suppose that single act would net numerous amounts of opportunities that would create an enrichment of my life? You bet. The power of personal energy should never be underestimated.

Science has shown us that we have what is called a Human Energy Field. Our personal field is unique to us. This energy field is sometimes referred to as our Aura or our essence. Each of our energy fields are saturated with the most intrinsic and powerful information one could ever need. We are able to create absolutely anything and everything we desire and of course quite a lot of us do. We are able to create the perfect lifestyle which is befitting our purpose and of course quite a lot of us do. So the question is, why is it that the majority of us do not know how to consciously utilise our own information field which holds the key to our innate power? We are sitting in all the information we could ever possibly need, yet we have not yet learnt to consistently tap in to it in a conscious and deliberate way. Why is that? The answer must lie in the lack of knowledge and the lack of application of that knowledge. Do you agree it's time to upgrade?

# Chapter Two – Who Are We?

I am going to ask you a question and I want you to take it literally and seriously. Who do you think you are? Stop a second and try to intuitively feel the answer.

Do this exercise: Get a friend to ask you that question. You are only allowed to give them one word answers. Get them to keep asking that question over and over again until you start saying things other than what you materially and mentally identify with. What other words are starting to come to your mind? Keep going until you have exhausted your personal and foundational vocabulary. When you are surprised with the answers that start appearing in your mind, write them down. You can even post them on the Global Infinity forum. www.globalinfinity.co.uk. Let's start a consensus on what our real identity is.

You see on a deeper level we really know who we are. We have just been conditioned to think that our identity is what we do, what we acquire and what we are told. Nothing is further from the truth than what we intrinsically feel we are. When I ask this question to my children, they always come up with incredible intuitive answers like "I am everything you see." Our conditioning starts when we are babies. We are told what, when, where, why and how we are to do things and this is when we begin to construct the Who.

Many years ago I was sitting in a bookstore waiting for an appointment I had made with a young gentleman who wanted to work with my personal evolution company. I always try to meet people in book stores because I find it inspiring and I am a bit of a book junkie.

However, on this day I felt really too tired to browse through the new esoteric books that were out on the shelves. So I played a game. I sat down heavily on one of their sofas and faced the rows of books that I was interested in. I asked the universe to point out a book that it thought would be relevant to my learning at that moment in time. I waited. As I started getting bored with the game my head turned towards a book on past life experiences. I was so not interested in that topic because I have always thought that it is better to look forward than dwell on the already happened past. I didn't even bother to get up to look at the book, which all of a sudden had an attractive cover.

I turned my head around and quietly said to the universe, Try again. It did. It made me look at another book on past life experiences and it was by the same author. Clever marketing I thought; make them both look attractive and appealing and someone might buy both at the same time. Can't fool me!! I stood up and looked in the other direction to see if a book would magically fall into my hand. I touched the books with my eyes closed, thinking that when I opened my eyes, the divine Book would suddenly fall into my field of vision. As I swung around with my coat over my arm trying to let another reader pass, I accidentally knocked over a book. I picked it up and it was that blasted book that I had initially dismissed. I read the title – The Journey of Souls by Dr. Michael Newton. I still wasn't interested so I placed it on the side. You know what? It fell off the side!! This is when I stopped and thought of my original intention to find a book befitting for me at this time and moment. I read the blurb at the back and I felt a rush of resonance. My whole body literally shivered. For me, when my body responds in this way, I know something profound is happening which, at that moment, is perhaps beyond my conscious understanding. What I read was different from just the normal past life experience. It was a clinical hypnotherapist's research with his own clients about what happened to you and your awareness at the point of death in your past life till the moment of reincarnation in your current life. It was an account of life between lives. What really did go on in the afterlife? I was flabbergasted and intrigued, as I always sensed there was information that was missing concerning the other side of 'death'.

There was a reason why I was now very interested. One day, over the summer period of that same year I had a moment of darkness. You know the feeling: despair, confusion and loneliness. I had the strongest feeling that I wanted to go back home. However, I had the sense that home was not actually a location on this planet. It was a location somewhere else and that's where I intuitively felt I wanted to be right at that moment. It seemed that this place was a place that I was missing terribly but I couldn't quite grasp it. So this book that wouldn't let me go was about to tell me what happens to people the moment they die to the moment they come alive again in a new incarnation. Intrigued, I knew I was about to follow a journey that would make concrete my suspicions of self and rid me of a layer of egocentric, conditioned nonsense that had been my armour of self protection. In short, I was willing to re-experience my death in order to be more fully alive.

A few months after reading and digesting the book, I was even more intrigued and highly excited. I decided that the Supra-conscious therapy that Dr. Newton's clients underwent would be a great insight that I wanted to include in my workshops. I believed that it would greatly enhance the sense of universal oneness and purpose of each and every one of us on this planet, and to me that meant speeding up the process of human evolution. A vital process in this day and age!! I rang Dr. Newton and asked him to take me through the process. Although willing, he said it would save me time and money to have the process done with Dr. Andy Tomlinson, who was trained in the Newton method and furthermore, was conducting research of his own on the subject of life between lives. So, I jumped in to my car and drove down to Dorset to reveal who I really was. What I was about to experience was to give me an unalterable experience, a headache and a major enlightenment. I was blown away with the amount of unified information and literally out of this world knowledge that I apparently already knew. I was carrying this information around wherever I went. It confirmed my passions, my purpose, my focus of how I create my wealth, my health, and my relationships. Most importantly, it revealed to me specifically why certain people were part of my life and the messages I needed to hear and learn to spiritually grow. I experienced others who I recognised and at the same time didn't recognise on this earth. I felt a sense of profound knowledge and most of all a profound sense of love and protection and security.

I knew, without shadow of a doubt, that I was on the right path in this current life and I now knew why people said I looked as though I was being channelled whenever I spoke on stage to a public audience. At the end of my incredible four hour session, Dr. Andy Tomlinson, who also had a strange headache, decided to add sections of our session together in both his books, in which he was researching deeper levels of conscious awareness: *Healing the Eternal Soul* and *Exploring the Eternal Soul.*

Know one thing: we are most definitely spiritual beings having a human experience and to experience that truth one need to experience that realm. The paradox is that we visit this realm every single day and we don't recognise it. We consistently miss our opportunity of personal power. This begs a deeper question. If we are all spiritual beings and we know without a shadow of a doubt that what we experience when we die is pure unadulterated love and guidance, then why are we here? What is the purpose? And how do we reveal that purpose individually? Our common purpose is to display the wonderment of Being in all its colours, shades and hues so we can experience evolvement on a spiritual level. We are ONE consciousness and creation has already been done. There is nothing else to do but manifest it in ways beyond our current imaginations.

## You are Phenomenal

So now we know. Our bodies, personalities, egos, etc are basically tools we choose in order to serve us as we learn the lessons of our journey as spiritual beings. We perfect our essence through how we manage and manifest our health, wealth, relationships, business, and careers. Once we know the foundations of who we are, we come to realise that our destinies are just a matter of conscious creation.

You are not merely a Human Being... You are far greater and more powerful than that. You are a magnificent, creative and expansive Spiritual Being displaying the power of your manifestations in the very notion of your existence. You are consciousness itself, the infinite all of everything there is. You are the Buddhas, the Mohammeds, the avatars the Jesuses. You are nature. You are ALL of it and you command the universe and everything in it with the notion of self. In short you are phenomenal. How powerful is that?

It is so important to understand this point because if we try to reach an understanding through our limited view as through the eye of the human perspective, our journey to enlightenment will take us much, much longer, but then again, maybe that is your particular purpose.

So right now, do this: Get a friend and ask them to read this section out to you. It is a matter of experience and there is no time like the present to start experiencing yourselves now.

Pick up a piece of fruit or your favourite snack, something that makes you feel good eating. Take a bite and close your eyes. Notice how your mouth starts to salivate as your salivary ducts secrete saliva which will mix with the food you are eating. Notice how the food is getting wetter and softer as you chew. Now eat even slower. Notice the action of your jaws going up and down and slightly around. (If you are still reading give the book to a friend or family member and start participating in the exercise. Get them to do the reading). Be very aware of every action that is taking place as you perform this action. Notice your posture, your breathing…notice your hand positions, the positions of your legs. Notice the way you feel, the sounds around you, the warmth or coolness of the room.

Now notice the being that is observing you. Aware of you, your physicality. And if you are aware that you are being noticed by you, which one is the real you? The physical or the awareness? If it is the physical that you feel is the real you then turn around and look at your awareness and say hi. Where is your awareness located and what does it look like? If it is your awareness that is the real you, greet your body and marvel at the actions it undertakes when you want it to. Look at it from above and describe your body in detail. Is your physical body in full control of your awareness? Or is your awareness in full control of your physical body?

Once you have fully identified with your awareness, pick up the book again, allow your awareness to expand whilst you are reading the words. Allow your awareness to evaluate what you are about to absorb and feel the information rather than intellectually taking it in. That way you allow your awareness, which is connected to the divine, to make your decisions using your physical senses to navigate it to the truth. We can never get to personal transformation through intellectual knowledge. Our transformation begins with emotionally understanding our foundation of self, and thus the very concept of who we are.

To reiterate, we are here on earth to manifest the abundance we have already witnessed in other dimensions right here on earth. We are powerful creators. We are here on this earth to play and have fun, to witness our beauty and to experience the love from whence we came. We are here on earth to learn and grow and to experience our magnificence.

So why does that ideology hardly ever get played out?

Well, it is purely because our vibrational frequency on this plane is much denser than our supra- conscious awareness. Earth has a frequency that is beautifully dense, creatively malleable and elegantly powerful. It displays characteristics which challenge our frequencies whilst we are incarnate. And to be challenged is an energetic evolution on to newer and bigger and more beautiful creations.

When we first incarnated on to this plane, it was quite difficult to navigate the physical senses of the human body. The density of the energetic matter that you would call skin bone blood, in essence the body, was such that one was spiritually inclined to 'forget' the power of Self in order to concentrate on the navigation of the newer bodily encasement. An exciting period of learning began. We never really forgot though. It was just that our focus had to be on navigating a denser type of frequency. Our challenge is to find ways to reveal our higher frequencies of consciousness or self awareness through the denser materials of the earth's biosphere - and that is the learning! And still is the learning. It is incredible because each and every time we incarnate on this earth we discover new ways to express the beauty of the natural self. Each individual has a specific and particular way of creating their journey and this is not only a gift but an essential component of soul evolution. Our goal here on earth is not to achieve personal gain and fortune; that is irrelevant, for we already have all that we need. Our goal is to achieve soul enrichment for a new dawning of being.

## Technology

Is it any wonder that we invent the most miraculous of technologies with seemingly no effort at all? We leap and accelerate at a breakneck speed in science, technology and the media and our efforts seem always to want to expand and go beyond thought and time. We seem to sense our purpose in almost every advancement we make and at times we touch that space of completeness and we align ourselves to the ecstasy of the moment, the moment of full knowledge of soul self. But still the fine threads of being are challenged to penetrate the density of the physical being in order to recognise that pure state and keep it constant. So the game continues. We go further than we have ever done, become better than we have ever been, and fly higher than we have ever flown, whilst we are constantly upgrading the tools and technology we use in order to get this far. And all of this is just an expression of the divine self inherent in each and every one of the 6.7 billion bodies that walk this earth. In a material sense, we know that we came in to this world with nothing and we will leave with nothing, so what are we doing in the interim? What exactly are we waiting for? This book is designed to hopefully give you clarity on our individual purpose and that of the collective.

This human body has been designed to such an extent that it has allowed us the power of exploring its realms in all its capacities at our own free will. In so doing, we have effectively allowed our bodies to accept what we know in the physical realm as truth and have put to the back burner information that we instinctively know in the energetic realms. Can you see how intricate the game is? This was surely a necessity in order to master the realm of the physical so we can better understand how we can align our frequencies in the most exquisite of ways to manifest our knowledge of light. Our amnesia has allowed us to indulge in all sorts of activities, frivolities and categories of dense thought that we label and catalogue in order to up the ante of the game. In our complete awareness, we know full well that that there is no such thing as right or wrong, good or bad, evil or heavenly, for that is the human frequency of language. We know for sure that these feelings that we perceive in the human body are the nature of different energy frequencies that vibrate within us at any one time.

When we take a bird's eye view of human existence, it is ingenious the way we as humans organise ourselves in to social groupings according to our larger and smaller soul groups to create types of learning that will get us closer to our goal.

The learning comes from accepting that we all journey in different ways and that we could all fit our different ways in to a gigantic universal puzzle if we changed our perspectives of self. In the western world and thanks to quantum theories, these learnings are now being adopted. The learning that we in the west failed to accept for thousands of years are now just emerging in this atomic age and we are perhaps in the most crucial stage of soul development than we have ever been in this particular run of human evolvement..

It is great when we are living in the human perspective, but now it is time to push ourselves a little in to the awareness of our powerful innate ability of higher conscious manifestation. Are you ready to push the boat out a little so we can reverse the tides of change that will surely come if we don't wake up in physical time? It is great that we human beings are self replenishing (we stand at nearly 6.7 billion people on this earth at the time of writing) but it would seem a little wasteful of the efforts we have put in to know ourselves, only to destroy ourselves at our finest hour. We also need to be clear that our natural world is also us and thus we must find ways to beneficially incorporate it to support our ways. That fact that most human beings have a strange disconnect to the planet and its beauty is a menacing ideology which will effectively destroy what we know.

All of our energy seems to be pushed outwards in creating tangible comforts for our lifestyles. In fact as human beings, especially those who play the 'western game', we have developed our outside comforts so well that we can no longer deny the power of manifestation that is within us.

Extraordinary phenomena happen right in front of our noses and we stubbornly dismiss them. Science has come up with reams of data evidence and proof of our unfathomable and incredible abilities and we still dismiss it. We have tools that develop our brains to accept the higher frequencies of ourselves; so it's time to wake up. It is time for us to embrace our birthright and step into the infinite realms of pure conscious manifestation. It is way past time for a collective upgrade.

## Preparation for Manifestation - An exercise

Let's lighten up the mood and play a little by taking a look at our physical bodies and becoming familiar with the power of creation.

**Exercise:**
Before you begin this exercise read the whole of the exercise first. Then sit quietly for 10 minutes and observe your breathing. Breathe in slowly and deeply until your lungs start to take over the rhythm spontaneously. When indicated, you may if you wish play your favourite instrumental or meditation CD. Let's begin...

Imagine you have a magic mirror that allows you to look inside your body. You would discover a medley of magic and if you looked closer you would see that the magic was being composed by a unique orchestra of intricate energy fields that were suffused with highly organised and intelligent information that your conscious mind wouldn't even know how to begin to decipher. You would also realise that your energy field stretches beyond the magical mirror and beyond your imagination. What does this mean in terms of communication and the power of attraction? This intelligence is the source of everything and the source of your power is your individuated energy self; you have access to it at all times. Have you ever thought about consciously using it? After reading the whole of the next section put the book down, play your meditation CD and close your eyes or alternatively, ask a friend to read the next section out to you.

Use the power of your imagination to materialise a magic mirror standing in front of you. This magic mirror has the power to make you transparent and it can see every type of energy configuration and frequency that is inside your body and immediately outside. This mirror does not recognise weight and matter; it only recognises energy fields and form. What do you see in this magic mirror? What movements are you detecting? Look closer and see if you can find a matrix pattern. How many do you see? What do they look like and where are they located? What colours can you sense and do they have an intensity to them or not? Just observe and revel in the power of your energy and imagination. Note the kinds of feelings you get in your body when you observe the movement of the energy. What kinds of sensations are you experiencing? Can you detect weak points and strong points in your field?

If you notice any weak points, softly but firmly breathe into those weak points and watch as they glow brighter, just like blowing air onto embers to rekindle the light. See them get stronger and brighter. Know that these fields of energy are stronger and healthier than they have ever been. The energy filaments are as strong as the day you were born. Move inside your energy field and gently repair and replenish any area that you feel needs it the most.

Now look just outside your body form and note what you observe. When you are done experiencing your energy body, relax and imagine your body returning to its present physical form but more invigorated, stronger and replenished. Imagine feeling warm and strong, with your energy field protecting you.

Do this exercise every night and you will notice a huge difference in your vitality and health. Imagination is the most powerful asset we have as conscious human beings. Pushing the boundaries of your imagination stimulates the fields of energy and this is the beginnings of conscious creation. Start with your body. After all, it is the vehicle you have chosen to get around in.

## Sense and Sensitivity

Most of us are still only aware of the five senses we possess in order to navigate our world. We haven't yet learnt to focus on the multilayered communications that are innate within us. If you were able to see and sense your energy body and witness your breath changing the frequency of your field, energising it and perhaps healing it, then you have just used another powerful sense that is yours to use forever. Can you imagine how many other senses we have that we are not aware of?

According to one of the most phenomenal researches that was conducted late in the last century by Cleve Backster, it was discovered that the very act of your observation rearranges and reconfigures the very photons and structure of DNA in your body. Your imagination is the most powerful tool known to humankind, and the act of your focused observations creates manifestation beyond your current realm of consciousness. This is why it is time to upgrade our conscious levels and move into the realms of higher conscious creations.

When we place our awareness on the energy body, we discover that not only do our senses become more acute; our perceptions of identities start to change as we witness another dimension of ourselves. The more we practice these very simple acts of observation, the more we become conscious participants in the creation of our personal lives and thus the more directional we become.

In the past decade, 'new' scientific understanding has come up with undeniable evidential data and verification of our abilities. Try reading 'The Field' by highly renowned journalist Lynn Mc Taggart. Or Rupert Sheldrake's 'Morphogenic Fields' and one comes to understand that more and more new scientific information is shifting our paradigms of the self and that of the world around us. Classical Physics and Newtonian medicine is beginning to stall our progress as many of the scientific 'old' truths are either obsolete, non applicable or being upgraded. Therefore, our stubborn conditioning to hold on to old paradigms is slowing down the application of new ways of doing things. It really is not difficult to overcome these conditionings; it just takes patience, knowledge and practice to begin to understand how far you can push your personal evolutionary boundaries and transform yourself.

It is not long now before the effect of our amnesia will start to diminish and indeed in many places in the world this has already begun to take place. As we start to pull our collective perception into alignment with the increase of energy frequency due to our acts of emotional desires, we will begin to experience a massive shift in perceptual reality. This will coincide with the human perception of world disaster. Yes, the world will go through a detox; it is a cycle. And yes, the human perception of self will shift. In order for the shift to be effective, it must coincide with the energetic replenishing of the earth's bio system. In a way, and as we shift, disasters will not be seen as calamities but rather as learnt blessings. This shift will not only affect our past but also our future. This brings in a new phase and thus a new level of soul evolution. Many people will call this shift many things, but by the looks of things, the shift has already started and we must embrace it.

## Personal Paradigm Shifts

Now is the time to start putting our full potential into force and begin to banish all of this nonsense. If you instinctively know that in your lifetime there will be a huge change for the better, then you have already begun your personal shift towards our role in global transformation. If you are still in doubt, then you are still thinking in the paradigm that created our current earthly situation. We are the ultimate creators of experiences and it is definitely in our power to think and feel a different way in order to create a different world.

So how do we do it? The answer lies within our immediate energy fields that have been surrounding us from the moment we became physical. Isn't it funny that in the western society we have duped ourselves so well by the very nature of our quest to know how our world works, that we have not fully recognised that we are in fact the very portrait of what we seek. Everything we ever wanted to know about ourselves and our world is situated back at home, the Source manifested into a physical structure – the Human Being. We have never left home, it just looks and feels different – but, for a moment. And that moment has been our window of opportunity which has never closed.

There are very few people on this planet who consciously use the powerful properties of information and energy to create the upgraded version of the newly evolved human being. However, the pace is picking up and soon we all will be enraptured with a new delicious paradigm in which we are all the pioneers of a conscious new world.

Such a shift happened to one of my delegates who came to a workshop I was conducting in London. This young lady was full of self recrimination, hatred and despondency. She believed that the world was out to punish her and everywhere she looked she saw accusatory eyes, mean faces and experiences that she braced herself for, knowing that they would be detrimental to her. This lady, whom I shall call Jane, felt suicidal. She knew she had a very negative outlook on life but she also reasoned to herself that she had proof for seeing life that way. Everything she did in life validated her feelings of self loathing.

After the first day of the workshop, I explained to her that her life was mirroring her emotions and thoughts, and the intelligent field that we are made up of was giving her exactly the experience she ran in her head over and over again. She said that each time she had an argument with someone, she would replay that argument in her mind over and over again with different variations and with more ferocious words. Words she felt she could or should have said at the time but didn't. Inevitably, she knew her script so well that next time she encountered a similar situation, out came that very same script and she would satisfy herself that at least she 'let that person have it this time'. Moments later she would feel despondent, desperate and convinced that the world hated her. She started losing friends, her work colleagues stopped trying to console her, her family were fed up and she began to feel worthless. Her life was spinning out of control.

This woman is a powerful creator of circumstances and she didn't even know it. The power of absorption was her trigger. The moment she absorbed herself in to a persona that was experiencing the very things she didn't want to experience, her energy field automatically communicated her powerful emotions to the Universal Source Blueprint

(USB). Instantly, and without prejudice, her concept of herself resonated with stuff that matched her emotions and graciously gave the experiences back to her. She did it again and again and again and the USB gave it back to her each and every time. It was like the USB said, 'Voila, you played this film over and over in your head and we now understand that it is real, so here it is. Your wish is my command'. How clever!

At the time we met, she refused to believe that she was the creator of her experiences and abdicated all responsibility. She soon realised that if she did not take responsibility for her own unique power, then she would just fall prey to what she perceived as life giving her bad deals. Besides, who wants to hang around people who feel bad all the time- unless you are the type who matches and resonates on that type of frequency as well? Slowly but surely she got fed up with herself and decided to change her approach to life. She made a conscious decision to wake up and FEEL happy, no matter what day it was and go to bed remembering something that made her happy. Eventually she started to reflect a different concept of herself to the world and the world responded in kind which opened up a few unexpected opportunities for her. One of the opportunities was that of living in a different country. She took up that offer and her life has changed unrecognisably. So how did that shift exactly happen? The answers are not secrets at all...

Personal transformation is accessible to anyone who is passionate about seeking freedom. Freedom to choose from the infinite array of possibilities your heart desires.

It is a freedom that you commit to consciously. I use the word conscious because we are all creating and manifesting on an unconscious level anyway. The trick is to be aware of what we do exactly and bring it to the forefront of our consciousness.

We are in fact at the point of understanding how we actually manifest abundance or otherwise. And once we understand the process fully, magic starts to happen and like with anything else, the pace quickens as our excitement increases. Then one day we truly wake up and our world has changed forever!

As human Beings we have the ability to do anything and become anything we like. We are nothing but pure potentiality. Some of us understand that we create our reality every step of the way. We create our outer world every minute of the day and we can create our inner world to match the exuberance that we call reality.

However, some of us scream out, "No, no, no! I am not ready yet to experience the exuberance of my power. I need to work out some old Karma that is plaguing me". Hey, that's all good too; we don't want to rush anyone. But don't forget your Karma is also a state of mind. You can realign yourself to any point of experience at any moment of time.

So in saying that, if you are still not resonating with anything that has been said since the beginning of this book, then, gently say, "No thanks. See you later." Put the book down on a shelf where you can see it every day and then go about your daily business as though you haven't even read a word. Remember, it is always at the point of giving up that those insights and revelations appear!

You see, synchronicity is a funny thing. It is another tool of emotional creation. It is the product of your intelligent psyche. And if you do still have this book in your hands, then you understand that this book was not picked up by you as a notion that was instigated by pure chance. It was a demand from your intelligent energy field relating to your personal quest which in turn is intrinsically entwined with your life's purpose and that of others.

Did you feel a sensation just then? If you experienced a high rush or a tingly sensation coursing through your body right now, then know that what you have just read is a truth and you are about to begin your miraculous journey of this lifetime. Your evolutionary purpose gets better from here, for you are about to realign yourself to your soul's purpose. We will talk more about recognising that truth of informational resonance in chapter 3, but right now let's just continue talking about how magnificent you really are!

## Wealth Is You

In this day and age, more and more people are feeling the unavoidable rush for the search for truth. They go from pillar to post to find that meaning, hardly giving themselves time to be still and listen to the truth that is resonating loud and clear from within their very essence.

Time and time again I see people run from one course to another, looking to see if they can find wealth, a healthier lifestyle, and keener prowess in finding the right relationship and so on. They eagerly grab on to anyone's strategy to create the experiences of their lives without stopping to think about what they are truly passionate about. After a few months, when their folders from the workshops have gotten dusty, they reminisce on the times they had there but their situation is still exactly the same.

I have worked with great wealth creators who are famous for becoming wealthy and having fabulous lifestyles. I have witnessed hundreds of young and elderly folk throw thousands of their hard earned cash just to get richer in the same way their 'hero' got rich. What people fail to see is the power of wealth lies within them, not in the strategies that these gurus purport.

Understand that their particular passion and strategy may not be YOUR strategy or even your passion. This indicates that most people look outside of themselves to create their lives instead of listening to the powerful intelligence that is already within them. Again, this is a conditioning that tells us to trust others more than we trust ourselves, in the sectors of health, wealth and relationships. All it takes is for us to listen to what we know is our passion. The moment we identify our passion we will recognise our purpose and it is at this moment that you begin the creation of your mission. Your passion, purpose and mission is where you wealth lies, and this is when the abundance of unimaginable proportions starts to kick in.

# In Search of Self

This calling or search for self is due to our biosphere raising its frequency, therefore creating a shift within our perceptions of self. How timely, considering we are supposedly in the midst of environmental catastrophe. However make no mistake, we as spiritual being are not caught up in the swirl of ego and therefore it must be understood that environmental chaos plays an important part in our soul evolution. Think of it this way: sometimes it take a massive big jolt to awaken the spirit to the next evolutionary level; it has been evident on an individual basis, with Near Death Experiences, that the person involved suddenly awakens to the truth about self and therefore begins to live their lives with a new perspective. Events that are soon to unfold on earth could be an evolutionary wake up call that serves a deeper purpose. These events are not to be looked upon as terrible acts of God, or even poor human error; they are cycles of learnings from which we choose. In a way we are readying ourselves for a new revelation and that is why so many of us are feeling restless as the intuitive resonance of knowing starts to draw nearer to a more complete form.

All of our acts of creation are divinely orchestrated. When synchronicities of any measure occur, it is part of the energetic multilayer of communication which is instantaneously broadcasted within the Universal Soul Blueprint of consciousness. To the person who is not aware of his or her own powerful part in co-creation, these synchronicities look and feel like strange and unearthly coincidences that bear no relation to self. But the contrary is true. In other words, you are the creator of the divine orchestration and you experience them on the level of the human perspective.

For so long, so many incidences that are anomalous to our everyday experiences seem to be kept outside of the realms of human acceptance. Therefore the power of manifestation is attributed to an almighty, all powerful, single, male source which was deemed to be separate from the human in the absolute. Religion is an understandable human perception and the perception is not the whole picture. Yes, there is a single source from which the human being is wholly part of and yes that single source did create the synchronicity and that single source is you!

At the beginning of the book we talked about coincidences. We now know that coincidences are information riding on energy fields that match our own emotional energy fields. Have you ever had a synchronistic event that made your mouth drop open and say, 'WOW, that was really freaky'? What did you do with that experience? I bet you told a few people, marvelled at it for a while and then passed it out of your mind. Did you know that if you took careful note of that synchronicity and matched it to your thoughts, you would have perhaps perceived an eerie sense of recognition or a falling into place of something? Perhaps an intuitive knowing of manifestation? If you looked at that synchronicity with a different perspective and found meaning in it, you would discover that the synchronicity was in fact a stepping stone to your goal, desire, mission, purpose or destiny. Furthermore, YOU created those synchronicities. You pulled them in to existence. You manifested them! Effortlessly! Does that make you the creator? You bet! How powerful is that?

There are times when we are thinking about a long lost friend and wondering what they are up to. Then the phone rings and, "Oh my goodness, I was just thinking about you", you say. Well, I was just thinking about you too. Well, who was thinking of whom first, and what caused this ticklish phenomenon of synchronicity? Just the other day, another one of my delegates, who is a PhD in Medicine, relayed a fascinating story of this particular type. She was thinking of another doctor that she hadn't seen in years and wondered where he was and what he was up to. She decided to stop procrastinating and she found his number and dialled. The phone was picked up immediately by the said doctor. Within minutes they established that the long lost friend had at that very moment her number in the palm of his hand ready to ring her! Both of them had lots to talk about and a new level of friendship began.

Early in the morning the other day, I had a very clear, lucid dream. The dream was vivid and pleasant and I was quite aware that I was dreaming and wanted to prolong the dream as long as I could. All of a sudden my mobile phone indicated that a text message had come through and the noise brought me back to a normal waking state. I instantly knew it was the person in my dream, but why should he be texting me at 7.30am on a Sunday morning? Very unusual. Of course to prove my self right, I picked up the phone and looked at the name of the sender. Lo and behold: it was my friend. I was tickled by the level of certainty I had and the fact that his thinking of me bled in to my dream, alerting me to the fact that he wanted to communicate with me. Did he feel that I was dreaming of him, which prompted his text, or did I pick up his intention to communicate with me, which prompted my dream? I think in this case he initiated the communication as the text was all about a business deal he was about to venture into!

We get these incidences all the time and it is truly a message from your inner self trying to gently wake you up to the fact that you are more remarkable then you have been led to believe and that you are living in a realm of multilevel communications. This is all geared to help you carry out your most spectacular purpose in life.

So what is that purpose? First of all, let's begin by putting ourselves on a pedestal. So do me a favour. Stand up on the nearest chair (don't do this if you are driving), pat your back and say, "Well done" for getting this far in our journey together. Go on, relax and let your hair down – get up on that chair and make someone giggle. Life is surely about living!

# Chapter Three – The Golden Pedestal

No one deserves to be on a golden pedestal more than you. You are truly amazing and what's more you are beginning to recognise it and that is the beginnings of personal transformation. Recognise that you are a person to be honoured - but the very first person who must honour you is you.

Anytime you sincerely want to make a change, the first thing you must do is understand who you are at the most fundamental level. To know yourself it is to understand what makes you tick, what powers you, and presses you to do the things you do. Are these ideologies really coming from yourself or are they visions of yourself that others have unwittingly placed upon you?

It is imperative to place yourself in a higher realm of importance, feel it and stick to it. Know that you are capable of doing remarkable things. When you know your abilities, your capabilities, your passions and that which makes you tick drive you to a point where you begin to experience them. Self projecting yourself on a global scale will only be a matter of time and nothing can take away that power you reveal to the world.

Every human body on this planet has a special gift to give to the world whether you are acutely aware of it or not. Most of the time we feel that we have not reached our potential or that there is something that we must do in or lives but we just can't get to grips with what it is in our lives. In a human perspective it is up to each and every one of us to seek out what that gift is within ourselves and project it. It is this gift that will allow others to want to learn how to shine theirs and it is also important for soul evolution. Wealth, happiness and abundance can only truly derive from your deepest desires. It will never come from emulating those who display their own power and make you think that that is the only way to do it.

One of the ways to understand what one's gift is to the world is to discover what makes you emotionally happy. Not just happy but ecstatically happy. What activity do you do that make you feel complete? Don't even think that you don't have an activity that you would do most willingly and without pay. Tonight, think back to when you were young, before you were told what was best for you to do. What did you spend most of your time doing or playing at? What was the first role you wanted to be in? What feelings did you enjoy experiencing when you were doing that certain thing? This energy alignment of pure happiness is encoded with rich information about what your true and natural gift is. It is your navigator. Your natural happiness whilst performing these activities emanated from your deepest desires and has the effect of attracting and affecting others. This obviously leads to opportunities, which in turn allow you to build the platform from which you will launch your gift and move on to your next step of soul evolution.

Recently I was coaching a woman, whom I shall call Melinda, who was attending one of my mentoring sessions. I asked her a question: "If you had one thing your life that you wanted to do or achieve or become, what would that be if you knew absolutely nothing could stop you? Melinda declared quite defiantly that she didn't have a purpose in life or any type of compelling vision. So I asked her what made her happy. She told me it was gardening, nurturing and caring for plants. I then asked her if other people felt happy in her gardens and she broke out in a beautiful lush smile and said, "Yes, of course!" She got it – her purpose was to bring happiness to her environment and her world by creating beautiful gardens that reflected her inner peace. The energy that is felt in her gardens makes people feel peaceful and tranquil. Do you think she could create inspirational gardens worldwide to spread her version of peace and tranquillity? You bet. That's wealth. She now has the choice to tap in to that wealth and create abundance for herself in anyway she wants. It's that simple.

Make no mistake, creatively revealing and displaying your

truth brings forth an abundance of personal power and self fulfilment, let alone an abundance of wealth. You see, one of the greatest properties of being foundationally in tune with yourself is the attraction of other things in your life that will become in tune with you. This is the story of resonance. You will discover that material and non material things seem to magically drop effortlessly into your lap without you even noticing.

One of the reasons why great visible and great non visible people get to where they envisaged is because they take on the quest of purposeful enlightenment. They intimately feel their life's mission and they know what they want to achieve in their lives. They are lucid, directional, focused and absorbed. They expect great things to happen and they assume the visions and emotions of their future before it has even manifested. Their drive comes from their desire to be what is in their mind's eye and nothing will deter them from their vision. When one is in this state of creation, forceful quantum processes start to powerfully take place and it is in this state that you must learn to be. It is in this state that your gifts begin to truly shine out to the world.

Elevating yourself to a new level of brilliance means that you honour and admire your existence on this earth. You treasure it and have the need to reveal your treasure to the universe. This allows you to state with confidence, "Yes, I am here and look what I've got." In declaring your greatness, you give other people the incentive to declare theirs and you put forth a beautiful energy field that magnetises people towards you, thus validating your creation and pushing you forward to new levels of thought and emotional creation.

To be in this state you must become the state of greatness itself. In other words, don't just think you are great – feel it. Walk around in it. Imagine what you would look like if the world looked upon you and knew you were one of the greatest people alive. How would you walk, breathe, stand, talk to people? Get up and do it now. Greet someone as if you were that great person everyone was talking about. Remember, the world loves you, so act as though you love it back. This may seem like a bit of fun and playing but what you are doing at this very moment is very powerful and extremely important.

This type of activity literally changes the information that you are emanating in your personal energy field. The feelings that you emote, be it serving or disserving you, literally create a specific type of frequency that is absorbed and utilised by your very cells. On a bio-molecular level, your cells take on these frequencies and carry on with their activities using and absorbing the new type of frequency. Your cell membranes, which are extremely intelligent, will either reject this new frequency because it is disserving to the cell and therefore the cellular system or it will find high use for it. Either way you will get feedback – your body will literally tell you whether this new frequency is serving or disserving.

The more you continue to be emotive with these feelings the more your cells and therefore your body will adapt and change. Your cells will literally emulate your emotions on a cellular level and emit these frequencies into your magnetic energy field. And guess what? As soon as your field is imbued with strong enough information energetically because you believe it, other people will start feeling AND believing that information upon that energy frequency that is coming off you and will start looking at you in a different way. They will start treating you in a different way. And they will start thinking about you in a different way. Most importantly, they will start to think about themselves in a different way – and that is the act of global transformation.

So then the saying is true: for us to change anything in this world, we must first change ourselves. I believe the majority of the world does not know exactly what that statement means. It is a powerful statement and it is a literal one. And that is exactly the purpose of this book: the process of transformation – your upgraded transformation.

Now that we have firmly planted ourselves on the Golden Pedestal, there are certain requirements that we must adhere to in order to take ourselves to the next level. These requirements are a must because they actually tap in to the field that activates the process of creation and manifestation.

**Expect the best of yourself.**
**Expect to get phenomenal results.**
**Expect to create and receive miracles in your life.**

Expectation is a powerful thing. When you expect something to happen and that expectation turns into a knowing that it will happen, consider your intentions done. Later on in the book, we will examine what it is you are tapping into that creates this reality, but for now take it as a given. Expect all that you want to happen and know that it has already happened.

When you expect the best of yourself, everything else that does not serve you seems to just fade away. Your focus is on the best result. We all have experienced times in our lives when we know for sure that we are the best at something. You feel on top of the world and you start to experience a roll of 'good fortune' that validates your expectations. The converse is also true. You expect something not too good to happen and then you have the bad luck of threes. It is even a coined phrase that we adhere to: 'bad luck comes in threes.' And yes, we allow it to enter our fields. Who in their right mind would want to expect two more bits of bad luck after they have already experienced one? What would make you want to put that on yourself, and then we even go looking for it! As you expect it, you manifest it and your intentions are done. Voila! You have proven again that you are the creator.

So if both great and challenging events can happen to you and you stood at the portal expecting all of that stuff to be delivered at your door as your chosen set of experiences, then it stands to reason that your power of creation even manifests when you are not aware that you are creating. Can you imagine if you were consciously aware that you were creating a certain aspect of life and you fully expected it to happen and you drove all your energetic power towards it by paying attention and KNOWING that it will happen? How powerful is that?

Expecting to get brilliant results is like knowing that they are yours to have. This knowing is intuitive and of course we need to practice it more. Often we get lucid visions of something being just perfect but we forget to remember what that felt like at the time of occurrence. If we could recognise that feeling all the time, then we would know when we're on the right track.

You create and receive miracles in your life every day without even acknowledging them. So now is the time to expect them consciously, with precision and certainty.

If we could do all of these things with the playfulness of a kitten but with the power of a tiger, then we would begin to understand the true nature of self.

## The Trigger

Everything that has been created and will ever be created has already been created. The only thing you have to create in your life is the map towards your destiny. The rest is done – well, all the complicated bits anyway. We now understand that we are powerful, creative beings and it is now important to understand what pulls our map together to become our experiences. How do we manifest within the infinite possibilities of divine creation? What is the trigger that starts the ball rolling?

The trigger is your intention.

I grew up in Manhattan, New York. I was surrounded by bright lights in the big Apple and I wanted to take a big bite – at the tender age of five. For me, the feeling of being 'up there' on the movie screen was a goal that I felt I was destined to achieve. I acted it out. I walked it, talked it, and dreamt it. I even declared it to my mother and she swiftly told me that it was not going to happen! Many years later and here I am, an international speaker (if not a star), on the stage and speaking to thousands of people. I'm up there. For sure I am not on the movie screen but the feeling is just the same. How did I get here? I'll tell you exactly how later on.

What is intention? And how do we direct it?

Intention is the instigator of creation. It is the playing field of infinite possibilities. It is the essence of everything. Intention is not just thinking you want to do something and you want to get it done. That's dull and often non productive. Intention is far more creative and potent. And every single one of us is the product of intention and by default we use, command and direct intention as we create our living reality.

## The Twinkling of Your Mother's Eye

Before you were even conceived, there was an intention to create which was so great, that it continuously rides on the information fields that surround us. This intention resides in all of us and procreation is an obvious cause. Your parents were stimulated to act upon a powerful force which resulted in your father shooting out millions of sperm, one of which would eventually penetrate your mother's egg. The intent of that one sperm must have been one of creation. If it wasn't then it would have sat back, kicked off its helmet, relaxed and enjoyed the warmth of its new home – well as a male, there's nothing new there. I'm only kidding. However, of its own volition and with the mix of the powerful chemicals that were present in the female egg, the ovum started dividing. Now how on earth did it know to divide? After a few weeks, more incredible stuff started happening. Do you think that your mother said to your father, "Oh, goodness gracious dear, it's 6.30 already, I must make the spinal cord and the nervous system before supper, and gosh I've got so much skin to manifest?" Nope, she carried on with her merry ways (except for a few discomforts) whilst you were developing in to a masterpiece. Your body in its minute detail was being created independently from your mother's conscious awareness of exactly HOW it was being created. Where was that intelligence coming from? And do you for one minute suppose that as soon as you were born all of that intelligent awareness suddenly disappeared? No way! In fact you are still swimming in it. Trillions of bits of information still surround and embody you. You are a walking universal micro chip with the ability to be the interface between subjective genius and objective creation. The awareness you perceive that translates all this information is consciousness itself - the vast being that is you. That's how powerful you are. And if you created you with the power of your intent, then you had a purpose. You wouldn't have created you for no reason at all, would you now? I don't think so. There was something that you powerfully and passionately felt you needed to do on this earth plane and that is why you decided to create yourself in your current body that is perfect for your purpose.

Now, I know there are some people in this world who still kick back and just sit around but believe me, they are the ones who keep asking what life is all about. Their USB is tapping.

Your original intention was of such a high frequency that one could say that it is universally pure but it needed to be felt experientially at a lower physical frequency. That is the power of intent. It is now up to you to find ways to manifest your intent on this physical plane for why else you would bother being here.

Intention is the trigger of the universe that creates a forceful ripple effect within the universal matrix of infinite possibilities. It is the product of the omniscient and omnipresent source. You may call the source whatever you like. If it is in the religious context then it might be God, Jehovah, Buddha, Krishna, and Allah. Perhaps if you are a scientist you may prefer to call this power the Field, the source, the implicate order, universal consciousness or the matrix. If you are a mystic it might be the cosmic plane, the cosmos, and if you are none of the above, then it is a mysterious inexplicable power that just is.

Intention is the creative force that is at the crux of our being.

So if we know now that we have all originated from that vast field of infinite intelligence, the energy field that was infused with intent and purpose, then as we sit here right now, we are still infused with that intent and purpose. What is your intention? What is your purpose? These are the fundamental questions we have forgotten to ask ourselves when we get lost in our physical reality. But don't worry, you are going to answer these questions for yourself much later.

We have created ourselves in various forms that have expressed themselves in a trillion different ways. So therefore, right at this very moment, each and every one of us is a creator and we have the ability to create what ever we want. What prevents us from doing so are our beliefs about reality and the dramas we are willing play out as we lock ourselves in a three dimensional, time/space, singular reality.

So again, if we are that infinite and powerful energy of the Source, then we are not our bodies which we created. Our bodies are the illusionary, dense temples in which we reside. If we are not our bodies, then we must have the infinite intelligence and ability to heal the very bodies we created because we are extremely intimate with them. We know every nook and cranny of our bodies because we devised them – the knowledge of how to repair our bodies is in-scripted in our energy system. (So the baby did come with an instruction manual after all - on proviso that he remembers it has been there all along!)

When we intend something, it is so powerful that hardly any of us stop to consider the consequences of our intentions. We literally affect each other and the world, thus creating a reality that we so thinly perceive.

Intention precedes thought. The Universe responds to our

most intimate secrets and it is no wonder that there is a Chinese proverb that states, "Be careful of what you wish, for it may come true". This Chinese proverb is alluding to the intention behind the wish and don't forget, a wish has more force of emotion than a thought. We have all experienced saying something that we didn't really mean after we've already said it, but nevertheless the intention was still there, and the intention was at its strongest just before the words flew out of our mouths.

Our thoughts transform in to words. When we have a true thought it is in fact made up of energy. This energy has a higher frequency than the energy of words that come out of our mouths, another vibratory frequency, (Hmm, a new perspective on the phrase "talk is cheap"). What does this all mean? Well, in terms of manifesting an outcome, our thoughts have precedence over our words, whether we see our thoughts in words or pictures. You can talk up a storm but if your true thoughts are incongruent with what you say, then your talk is just a puff of noise holding no creational weight. In that respect, we really are what we think. Here's another saying for you, "The slip of the tongue is no fault of the mind" - have you heard that one?

But we can do even better than that. Our intentions actually precede our thoughts because in order to formulate a thought we would have to have had an intention, a feeling or desire which created the thought in the first place, a purpose, and a driving force that stimulated our thinking. So our intentions have an even higher vibratory frequency than our thoughts and this means that our intentions have precedence over our thoughts.

It is these intentions that get pushed out into the universal consciousness. Do not forget that we are all part of the universal consciousness (because we too are made of just different oscillating frequencies of energy) and we communicate with it every moment of our lives. However, the currency that gets registered in the cash till, so to speak, is your intentions and it is at this point that you can 'purchase' your dream destiny. To put it another way, you can intend anything you want in this world and you can be sure that sooner or later you will definitely get it, providing that you align your energy with that intention consistently.

My parents decided I was going to be either a doctor, a lawyer or an account –certainly not a movie star. I couldn't understand how they could choose for me; surely they chose for themselves, right? Well, after failing chemistry abysmally and having no interest in the law whatsoever, I ended up at university studying a European Business Degree. I remember having to prepare and give presentations to my tutorial groups and loving being in the limelight. In one particular presentation, my marketing teacher said, "Naomi that was a first class honours presentation. I can see you on television like Oprah Winfrey." Goodness, you couldn't wipe the smile off my face all day! However, that evening I became very confused. My old passion of being in the media raised its head again and I knew I didn't want to spend my life 'doing' business and economics presentations in boardroom meetings. What was I supposed to do now? A very dear friend of mine at the time suggested that I go and see a clairvoyant. When she saw my eyes roll upwards to the heavens, she harangued and pestered me nearly every day, claiming her life had been 'sorted' by this mystic.

Eventually I relented and accompanied her to a strange place in Shepherds Bush, London. There I sat down in front of a woman who had massively thick bifocals and a crystal ball! Oh boy, here we go, I thought. I am a student. I can't be wasting my money like this! This woman instructed me to put my energies on to this crystal ball by gently rubbing it and to only answer yes or no to her questions. I obeyed. She then proceeded to tell me things that anyone with half a brain could have picked up like: I have many friends, I am outgoing etc, etc. She then started to tell me things that she couldn't have known but were perhaps good guess like: I have family in the United States; I have two sisters etc, etc. She then proceeded to tell me things that she could not have known in a million years, like: You have been given an invitation to go to Argentina but you will not accept it. This little piece of information made me sit up and pay attention. I was baffled because just that week, my elder sister's friend told me that if I couldn't get into television by the end of the year after I had finished my degree, then she was going to ask her brother if I could work in his production company due to the fact that I spoke Spanish. He and his production company were in Argentina. I had told no one at the time because I didn't want my mother to somehow scupper the plan and here is this woman telling me I wasn't going to take up the invitation. The woman then asked me if I had anyone looking after my job interests and I said yes, (it was a lady from the secretarial agency). She then asked me if it was a man, and I said no. "Are you sure?" she said. "Yes", I replied. "Well", she said, "there is a man who is looking after your job interests and he is the man who is going to open the doors for you in the media world". My mouth dropped – and suddenly this woman was my best friend. "You will meet this man," she continued, "in the summer and once you have met him you must continue to keep knocking on the door. After that you will start to rise very high in the media industry and you will travel all over the world and be very successful."

I was breathless – she could see all of that in the crystal ball? I didn't hear much of anything else as I was plotting my future already as I was looking forward to travelling around the world. I thanked her and gave her a grand sum of five pounds.

That was March. In June of that year, I and a few friends of mine decided to go on our last holiday together before we had to get stuck in to working the rat race. We chose one of the small islands in Greece and it was on one of our last days on holiday when some guy came up to me and started giving me 'the chat'. I was so totally not interested that I couldn't believe that he didn't understand my "go away" body language. After five more minutes of trying hard to seem polite, this young man told me that there was a guy in the bar from which he had just emerged, who wanted to meet me and would I accompany him to the bar. Horrified, I said absolutely not. I was quite comfortable with my friends outside the bar, thank you very much. He then declared that he was going to bring the other man out! Fine, I said. So he brought him out…

This man was much older than me but had a very confident and happy presence. As he extended his hand for a handshake, he looked me straight in the eyes and said, "Hi, my name is Steve Blame and I'm from MTV News". My initial bored countenance swiftly changed as my eyes popped out of my head and my voice turned sweet as I gushed, "Hi my name is Naomi and I wanna be a presenter; gis a job". It came out just like that. Steve chuckled and said he couldn't give me a job but he knew someone who could. So he gave me his telephone number and asked me to ring him when I got back to London. Was I thrilled? Hell yeah!

The most curious thing about this synchronicity is that Steve and I discovered that neither of us knew who that young gentleman was who introduced us to each other nor have we seen him since. Even more curious was the fact that he told us exactly the same lines in order to get us both to meet.

It is important to remember that your destiny has instantaneously been created the moment you intended it, literally! What happens is this: you feel a need to do a particular thing and you then throw out an intention into the universe. At that exact moment, your intention has materialized but in an energetic form. It exists! The trick is keeping your intention consistent and constant. You are not only the creator of your own destiny but you'll also influence others just by your intentions behind your thought processes. So be very aware of what you intend!

So how did my dreams of getting into the media manifest so quickly? I discovered a tool that might just help you manifest your dreams just as quickly. All will be revealed very soon.

# The Spotlight

When someone pays you a certain amount of positive attention, doesn't it feel good- especially if that attention was not solicited? Paying attention to anything has a miraculous affect on the object, bringing it to life by literally breathing energy- the source of life - in to it.

Paying immaculate attention is the second force in creating our destinies and thus accumulating abundance in our lives. Without it, abundance will easily slip away like water through your fingers. Synchronicities are the indicators which tell you that your intentions are being activated. It is imperative that you pay attention to them and use them as stepping stones toward your designed Destiny. If you do not pay attention to those synchronicities and recognise them when they arrive, another opportunity is lost and sadly, because most of us are paying attention to the things we do not want in our lives, then these events manifest instead. As a consequence, the great opportunities which lead us to abundant futures are lost time and time again, causing delays to our desires and creating frustration and unhappiness along the way.

Attention can be equated with energetic love. And I am not talking about sexual or family love. I am talking about universal love, the love that allows one to become and step into one's own, just by the nature of infusing it with the energy of attention. For example when a three year old child shouts out, "Look at me, look at me!" and you pay that child attention, that child, whether it is yours or a complete stranger, feels loved and therefore nurtured. If you do not pay attention to that child, and instead you tell them you are looking when you are not, then doesn't that child DEMAND the attention by calling you over and over again until you give them their due energy of love?

In fact, you cannot have any kind of meaningful relationship unless you pay attention to that person. It is the same with synchronicities; you cannot pick up the flag post clues unless you pay close attention to them, recognise them and validate them. The more attention you pay to synchronicities, the more they will appear as your acuity to them becomes sharpened. It's back to that common experience of wanting something which is new to you, hadn't noticed it before but now you notice it everywhere since you pulled focus on it. Again, we will talk about how to create this experience over and over again with the things that you really want in your life.

Paying any type of attention uses the universal fuel of energy. It could be as personal as being fully present and engaged when someone is talking to you, thus allowing them to clarify their thoughts and thus facilitating them to become more fluent in their thought processes and more articulate in their speech. Or it could be intangible, as when you are expecting a certain incident to happen and you deliberately look out for it, and never mind the probabilities, it actually does happen and thus validates your efforts of paying attention. Sharpening our skills of attention means that we are sharpening our faculties of observation. To acutely observe ourselves and our environment, knowing that we are expecting a result from our deliberate intentional creations means that we are playing the game we intended to play. We are playing within the realms of spirit rather than in the realms of physicality and conditioning. When we are able to consistently and proficiently sharpen our focus, we will find that we are able to direct our pools of energy to a particular person, object or outcome and again create the reality we perceive.

When you pay attention to something, you start to bring it forward towards you, and your energy system starts behaving like a magnet attracting like energies.

Remember this phrase: Wherever attention goes, energy flows.

Attention is so extremely important when creating your destiny because synchronised and coincidental events come in many different forms. As you build up your acuity through attention, you will find that your intuition will then start to kick in.

## The Navigator

You have a built-in navigator system that is superior to any navigation system that man could make. It is called intuition: ahh intuition, the knowingness of being. This is the supreme and vast information centre that helps you to navigate your choices in a sea of infinite possibilities.

What exactly is intuition? Intuition is the generic name for the profound sense of knowing a fact that one could not possibly have known by using logic, reasoning or formulation. Women and mothers especially, seem to experience the phenomenon of knowing, usually because their vibratory make up is more sensitive or in tune with universal intelligence. Do you remember a time when you had a queasy feeling about something and you didn't want to go ahead with the transaction/deal/contract? Logically, the deal looked good and sound, but intuitively you had a gut feeling that was almost making you feel sick. You wanted to call it off but your logical mind kept on telling you that you'd be crazy if you didn't go through with this, and everyone kept on telling you that this was a once in a life time opportunity, never to be repeated. But you still felt uneasy. Despite your feeling, you went ahead with the deal anyway and soon enough, it started to go wrong as the deal started to reveal and unravel itself. You screamed out to yourself, "I knew I shouldn't have done that, I just knew it." Well, if you knew it why did you do it? You see we all get these wonderful messages come from the highly intelligent part of ourselves but because we have been trained to think things out logically, methodically and systematically, we dismiss the natural messages of our intuitions. This is the battle between left brain conditioning and right brain creativity. Yep, time and time again, we wonder why we keep falling down the same trap every single time. It is mostly because you are not paying attention to your intuition which is connected to your higher intelligence – your energy field. The times when we do listen to our intuition - like cancelling a train ride because something didn't feel right or not going down a popular and familiar road because it just didn't look right, literally saved us from encountering something that could have been unpleasant. Our Human energy field assimilates and translates information from our environment and instantly sends an oscillating frequency to our physical bodies, which translates the information, stimulates our cells to produce the perfect cocktail of chemicals which in turn gives us a sensation together with an emotional response. That emotional response gets translated into meaning via our belief and value systems and then we know (the operative word here is KNOW) what action to take.

For some time, intuition was viewed as a mysterious and intangible part of the human psyche and indeed, in the western world hundreds of years ago, it was feared and reviled. One would be accused of heresy or be called a witch and burnt alive for displaying such knowledge. However, thousands of years prior to the Middle Ages, the world rejoiced in the wondrous intuitive knowledge and praised the 'oracles' or the 'seers' of the time.

Nowadays we are coming full circle and science has radically changed the views of many who seem reluctant to accept that we are more than our five senses. Indeed, to those of us who experience the power of intuition, science need not prove anything, for experience is a far more potent indication of truth then any double blind research experiment in a clinical laboratory.

Some people might call intuition the sixth sense, psi, supernatural abilities and many other terms besides. All of these terms allude to something that the ordinary person cannot be party to unless they have the 'talent' or a gift. Well, to put it bluntly, intuition is a NATURAL human ability; we are all already extremely skilled in it, we just haven't quite come to the age in positively recognising, perceiving it, developing or directing it.

Intuition plays an important part in creating our destinies because it helps us navigate our maps through the choices we feel to be right. Do you remember the saying, "If it feels good, do it?" Well that is true for intuition. If it feels right and it is coupled with a physical sensation, then that choice or information is very rarely, if at all, incorrect and if it does turn out to be incorrect, it is the meaning you have given it, not the information itself.

Having a gut feeling is an indication that your intuition is at work and it would be wise to pay close attention to what type of information is being conveyed. A foreboding feeling or indeed a feeling of anticipation or euphoria and excitement, is also an indication that some information is trying to get through to you. It is at this point that you have got to be prepared to 'listen', 'see', 'hear', 'feel' and 'taste' the message.

Other types of intuition can take the form of telepathy where we are able to 'read' other people's minds (note, you are not exactly reading what's inside their heads per se, you are reading the information that is hanging on their human energy field), as well as environments from the past, present and future. Remote viewing, where we are able to inwardly see a situation or an event that could also be in the present, past or future, has been recognised as a taught skill that absolutely anyone can do. Or precognition, where we are able to tell of events that are to come. These and more are part of our intuitive makeup. We all have these abilities. What is called for now is to make a decision on what you choose to focus on. Set the intention to bring your natural abilities to the foreground, pay close attention to how you feel and soon your intuitions will start blossoming.

Our bodies and the world resonate at the same vibratory frequency, so when you realign yourself with the universal intention, then you instinctively know the outcome. Your body instantly tells you by way of a vibratory rush up and down your body, a quiver, a quickening of breath or a full body shake. It is the entrainment of the energetic information that you feel. A coming together, a unity of source and self telling us that we are not alone: we are being, heard, felt and whatever is being asked has now just been given. You will perhaps feel excitement or anticipation or euphoria. That is when you know a truth or an intention has been registered universally. Don't expect the universe to adhere to your human notion of timing though. The universe is timeless and the paradigm of time as we know it will probably be the most challenging shift we will ever have to make in this lifetime.

You will also feel vibrant and alive. As you resonate your higher energy fields, you are literally sending out the message to the universe, to your fellow human beings and to the environment. Instantaneously, synchronicities start to occur as the universe conspires to grant you your wish.

Through our energy fields, we are also able to communicate without the aid of modern technology, what Dr Rupert Sheldrake calls Morphic Fields. This field allows us to use telepathy instantaneously - like birds when elegantly flying within their formations or shoals of fish when beautifully swishing in unison. We must then be able to see past and future events, but even more pertinent to us right now is the fact that we are be able to positively affect our universe through these invisible fields just by our thought processes

– and we do. There are many paradigms in which we live at this moment that dictate how we structure our thoughts. These universal paradigms hold a steady belief system that influences our thinking, whether we are aware of it or not. Therefore it is crucially important, especially in this day and age, to readdress our social paradigms in order for us to move on collectively and change the information encoded in the morphic fields. In other words, we have to change the way we look at things, change the way we see things and change the meanings we give to things. This takes a collective effort but it must start with the individual.

## The Human Portal

When one falls in love with the mystery of self, it is impossible not want to lie in the arms of the lover who offered you the right of knowing the essence of freedom. The bed in which one can find the intoxication of the lover is called meditation.

Meditation is your inner Time Out Zone, a place of solace, study, communication, love and unity. One is able to access all the information you need in order to create a powerful choice for the direction of your life. It is the sacred part of you, the beautiful vessel in which you navigate your life, for it contains your higher self and that of others to whom you are entangled. Meditation opens you up to the infinite amount of intelligence that is constantly present in the universe. It bathes you in its knowledge and indeed that knowledge is intuitively felt by you.

In our current western lives, we are suffused with

distractions that erect barriers to our desires of revealing our gifts. Mobile phones, television, MP3 players, ipods, general noise, etc all distract us from that powerful stillness that we know to be the true reflection of our vastness of self. It is incredible to know that some people are uncomfortable with or even afraid of silence. If one really wants to discover the pure headiness and beauty of the divine which resides within, then Meditation is not an option – it is a must. With a small amount of practice, one can fall into the lap of bliss and emerge as the ardent warrior of grace, fortitude and wisdom. How powerful is that? Meditation is a zone for gaining and submitting information and a zone for rebalancing the mind.

Those of you who contend with the idea that knowledge is power must understand that knowledge doesn't necessarily come from books, TV, newspaper etc. Of course these vehicles are great to gain other people's learned expression of reality; however, the real activation of knowledge comes in the form of self knowledge. Mediation is a unique and unrivalled platform from which one can obtain information that is truly pertinent to one's desires and goals.

There are many delicious ways to meditate: from walking in pure mindfulness, to sitting in the stillness of breathing, to dancing furiously within a mesmerising beat. All of these ways and much, much more are valid vehicles to laying down in the arms of the most luscious sense of ecstasy known to self.

Using your sessions of meditation as your main space of discovery will empower you with the knowledge of self,

self reflection and personal evolution. In time, you will begin to find your centre which is intrinsically connected to the nucleus of universal being, and when that initiation commences, your love affair with life begins.

When you come out of any state of meditation, it is important to come out slowly, bringing with you the sense of quiet and stillness that you have just been immersed in. You will probably come out with whispers of suggestions or insights or colours or patterns that may have meaning. Whatever information comes out, do not try to analyse it. Just observe and acknowledge what you have seen, heard and felt and then do or think of something else. At the right time, your subconscious will throw up a piece of information that will formulate in your conscious mind and you will have the opportunity to put it in to action. It is sometimes at this moment that some people get their 'Aha' moment.

The trigger, the spotlight and the navigator are the only tools you need to become a powerful and graceful creator. Practice using these tools and you will find that other senses of creations will begin to kick in naturally in order to pierce through the veil of unknowing, thus arriving within the realms of infinite possibilities.

## In The State of Power

Although meditation is a great place to be, I have found that there is another more powerful state, which I know without a shadow of a doubt is the key to my personal manifestations. When people used to ask me how it is that

I always seem to get what I want, it caused me to back up, pause and really think of what it was I was actually feeling, doing, seeing or being at the moment that I knew of as creation. I have no name for what it is that I exactly do but I know this is the key to my creation, so here it is:-

First of all it feels as though I go into a state of absolute stillness. It is like I am in a meditative state but the state is not meditative. It feels like I am in a state of heightened awareness or expectation. It feels like I am in a state of agitated but calm anticipation. In my mind, I am staring at the scene I want and I see it in minute detail. I still feel completely still, mentally, emotionally and physically. I know the actions, what is being said, even what is being felt. I have been told by friends who have witnessed me being in this state that it's as if I have zoned out and it is difficult to penetrate my concentration. One friend even said that she had to leave the room because the atmosphere was so intense.

I have no idea if others feel exactly the same way when they are in that zone but that is my experience and if it is of any use to you then please do take it as your own.

## Powerful Fields of Knowledge

All of us live in a coherent field of highly intelligent information. In order to understand who we really are, it is imperative to understand the fields of all our bodies, how our field feels when naturally at rest, what emotions come up within that state, what they relate to and how they work in unison to create our reality.

The human energy field is organized around emotions. And just like the fat molecules that wrap around toxins to keep them from harming you, so too does your energy if it recognizes that the emotion may result in a disharmonious energy configuration. When emotions become disturbed and distorted the energy field suffers, it becomes non coherent. This happens because the emotion gives the original energy field a signature tune or vibration. This vibration will continue to tap at the cells at a molecular level and transmit the vibration. The cell usually has a feedback loop in which it sends information to the energy field, telling it the results of that particular vibration. In turn, the body will get an alert information telling it to do whatever it takes to correct the 'fault' because it is non coherent to the cell.

However, quite a lot of the time, the cell is not able to give back the feedback information because the emotional vibration is too strong or violent, or the cell and/or body become weakened. The cell then tries to incorporate the vibratory information on a molecular level and as it does that, the cells regenerate new cells in a new configuration, which may be non coherent compared to the original field. This is when disease and illness occurs.

Now here is where it gets interesting. Our belief systems are emotionally charged. Everything we believe about ourselves and about our world has a vibratory frequency that charges and penetrates our fields of energy from the bio molecular level in our cells right through to the infinite objects that we are connected to in this earth and beyond. This has absolutely huge implications on what types of information we are putting out there and most importantly, what types of information we are gathering and processing in our everyday lives.

If you think about this fact closely, you will begin to understand that we have the power and ability to literally affect global transformation. You do it all the time and you have been doing it from time immemorial!

Every single thing you believe shows up in your life as though by magic. Some of us are acutely aware of this fact and some of us are completely oblivious due to our conditioned beliefs, but all of us have felt that uncanny phenomenon. This phenomenon happens because we have a real link to everything in our world and through the power of resonance, we vibrate that which we desire and then it appears.

The most important thing to remember is this: it is how we feel about what we believe that creates the powerful pull of manifestation.

According to scientists, we literally affect the quantum field by moving the sub-atomic atoms that make up the stuff of our universe. The language we use to communicate with our universe is that of feeling and observation. So, observe your feelings and you will observe your reality unfold in front of you.

We understand that our energy field is the powerhouse of our knowing. So how can we tap in to its abundance to reveal the beauty of creation on the physical plane? The answer lies in the quality of our field.

If our energy field has all the information that made up and powers our bodies, then the real intelligence does not reside in our brains but in our field. We must realise that our very DNA, which is a vibrational strand of information, derived its information from the field that created it in the first place. So it is not our DNA that runs our bodies, it is in fact our highly intelligent energy field. The interface to this huge amount of precise and divine information is the membrane of our very cells.

On an individual level, this is the field that surrounds the body which gets denser and denser the closer it gets to the physical body. Science, with its high technology, has detected many fields that emanate from the human body.

The first field of energy that immediately surrounds the body is called the etheric field, which is rich in information. This could be considered the blueprint of our physical being. The etheric field keeps our bodies functioning as the pristine machine it is. It adapts and corrects itself constantly, energetically feeding the physical body so that the heart beats in time, and the breath is continuous and the intricate functioning of the body performs beautifully without the attention of your conscious self. This is all done within the orchestration of the ingenious source.

Our energy fields have the property of magnetism. Therefore it also responds to gravitational forces. So not only will it align itself with the physical body but it will also align itself with your thoughts, your emotions, the environment and with other beings. Each and every point of your immense energetic field has an alignment with trillions of different points on this planet and beyond.

This is the reason why it is infused with billions of bits of information if not more.

Now imagine your etheric field navigating billion of bits of information, constantly filtering out information that does not serve it and keeping those which do serve it. The intelligence of your field is incomprehensible when looked at through human eyes. Your energy field will prioritise at any given moment in order to keep you at your best, even in the face of adversity.

This means that if anything disrupts your human energy field whilst it is flowing with energetic information, it will either correct itself or translate the information for the cells of the physical body to manifest the new information that has just come in. It will allow discordant energy configurations to manifest in the physical body only if a higher field is constant and repetitive enough for it to be forced to change its pattern. It stands to reason that the unique human energy field will try its hardest to keep the best coherent energetic information possible, in order to keep the body in the best health it can be in light of its environment, but sometimes this does not happen – why is that?

Other fields within our human energy field have also been detected, like the emotional field amongst others. This is a higher energy vibration and is linked with our thought patterns or our mental field, which is higher still. Whatever we think about and then give meaning to is then translated to our emotions. Our emotions serve as the navigational system of feelings, whether we like something or not. Our emotional field tells us whether we like what we have aligned ourselves to or not. It is as simple as that. If we don't like it, our intelligent emotional field tells us to move away from it. If we do then for sure we will move towards it and want more of what makes us feel good. The problem comes when we THINK we should like something but instinctively we know that we don't but we ignore ourselves anyway because we Think we know better. Hmm, it is starting to sound like we are making a Non Sense of our selves- literally not using our senses.

In essence, our energy fields have the power to correct the discordant energy configurations that cause illness in our physical bodies, to read information from all sources of energy imprints and to create other forms of energy information that manifest into physical reality.

One of the reasons why our energetic bodies are so important is that they are able to resonate with other fields of energy. In terms of health and healing, this is vitally important and in terms of consciously creating an outcome, it is the source of infinite power.

Isn't it true that there are times in our lives where certain things happen and we are absolutely puzzled by the circumstances surrounding the event? There are times when we know that our experiences seem impossible, crazy, and uncanny. We struggle to find ways to explain it but we cannot articulate it in any other way than to say that what we experienced was a sheer miracle.

Perhaps we were thinking of someone and they suddenly ring on the phone or appear at the door. Or we get a gut feeling about something or someone or a little voice in your head speaks loudly and clearly about a certain path that you should take. These are the 'coincidences' that point us in the right direction in accordance with our intentions. But if we look a little closer, we find that they are not 'coincidences' at all but information in the quantum field presenting us with messages, prodding us to take action and shape our destinies.

Every summer, my sister used to absolutely love going to Greece. One year, she brought back a picture of a very handsome man whom she had dated on holiday. My sister at the time had awful taste in men but this guy was something else. Both my younger sister and I were extremely impressed to say the least. I asked her if this guy had a younger brother and lo and behold she said actually he did and he was around about my age. Three months later, she took a trip to Italy to meet this guy and on her return, true to her word, she brought back a picture of his younger brother. The moment I took a look at that picture I knew instantly that this man was going to be the father of my three kids. I was certain of it. How did I know? I physically and energetically felt it. At this point he didn't know I existed on this planet.

Three years went by and my sister heard nothing of the brothers and suddenly the phone rang. My sister told me that my 'betrothed' was coming to England the following week for a month to study. He came and he never left and yes, he is the father of my three beautiful children! How's that for the Law of Attraction? We do have the capacity to create miracles!

# Chapter Four - Creating Miracles

So far, we have looked at what creates the stuff of miracles that manifests into our destinies. Now it is time to look at how all of that relates to us in everyday life. That is, how does one prepare to be upgraded? First, let's take a look at the body.

## The Body

Our physical world, the world of objects and matter, is made up of nothing but information contained in energy vibrating at different frequencies. This also includes our physical bodies. Each of our cells carries a vibratory frequency that is natural and unique to each individual. Each cell also carries huge amounts of specific information which correlates to specific functions within our bodies.

Like anything in this world, everything has an optimum working frequency, which allows an organism or thing to work at its utmost best.

Our bodies, like all other organisms in this world, have a locked-in Optimum Best Performance Frequency. So it stands to reason that we have a duty and an obligation to keep our bodies functioning like a well-oiled machine in order to get the best performance. Remember, the object of the game is to try to break through the density of the human form in order to reveal and make shine our spiritual selves. Keeping our bodies in great shape means our energy field is in great shape, and so too our minds and emotions. Yep, it is that body mind connection again - a point of Power! We have all experienced feeling sluggish at some point in our lives and that is directly due to the body feeling sluggish. The state of our minds affects our bodies and vice versa. Remember, the universe receives every bit of information that we send out – the postal system is our energy fields.

Obviously, any good health book will tell you that to keep your body healthy the best way is to nurture the body with what it really needs. So what does the body really need? There are seven basic essentials that the bodies must have in order to create a powerful field. Oxygen, water, fats, proteins, carbohydrates, vitamins, minerals and of course exercise.

Ingesting the above elements in the correct quantities, which are unique to your body, you will find that not only will your body function to its optimum, but you will feel great and look much younger than your years. I say this because time in terms of years is a human construct and doesn't exist. So what is a year? Nothing but experiences. So experience yourself as how you feel rather than how many years you have and you will discover that others will relate to your feelings in terms of deciphering how many years they think you possess. The greatest thing about having your body work in tiptop condition is that your energy field will start to emanate a powerfully healthy field. This is extremely attractive and people will literally be drawn to you. The Law of Attraction in motion. It gets even better: your perception of yourself and that of the world around you will change drastically and you will start to feel the same way as you did when you were of full of life. Have you noticed that young children suddenly break in to a run or a skip or a jump when they are just idly walking down the road? That is a sign of bountiful health in body, mind and spirit. Our bodies, as we gain more experience, are capable of staying that way so long as our lifestyles, nutrition and thought processes are in line and coherent with the physical needs of our bodies.

Looking at technology and borrowing from their ideology is a great way to understand how to upgrade ourselves. For the longest time, even though I had long past the 35 year old age bracket, I kept on being told that I looked much younger than my age. One check-out lady even asked to see my ID because she didn't believe that I was over 21! I attribute this phenomenon to me consciously feeling young. I never ever say, "Oh it's my age, I'm getting old you know." To me, that is paving your way to death as you instruct your cells to take on what old means to you. Neuroscientists have discovered that your brain gets old because it has not been given adequate exercise. Now in the stores you can purchase brain training games that exercise your brain and thus make your brain muscle stronger, which in effect reverses the apparent age of your brain. Now, as far as I am concerned, if you can do that with your brain, can we not do that with our bodies? Sure we can. Do you fancy setting an age barometer for yourself? Then hold tight and we'll get to that part soon.

I have always enjoyed good health and have never indulged in excessive abuse of my body. However, I discovered long ago that stress and sadness also strike a huge imbalance in the regeneration of optimal cell production. In that short period of my life, I had taken on too many projects and was struggling to mend a broken heart. I was so stressed that I did whatever I thought it took to get me through that period. So I drank too much coffee and wine. Ate far too few vitamins and minerals. Made sure I surrounded myself with comfort food and forgot that water was a liquid one drinks. I also allowed the anxiety and stress I was feeling to sabotage my breathing patterns thus leaving little oxygen for my cells to use and consequently allowing the cortisol levels (my very own stress hormones) to accelerate liberally around my body. Would you like to know what the consequences were of that lethal combination? Well, the very first thing I noticed was that everything was going wrong. Nothing was how it was supposed to be – my perception of life was becoming dark and gloomy. My skin became so alarmingly dry, that I literally sought medical help. A few more grey hairs turned up among my very black hair, and my eyelashes became so fragile that it looked like

I had none. My eczema returned with a vengeance and my energy levels just sank to rock bottom. Looking back at that time and knowing what I know now, I now realise that I was literally accelerating my death by each day that passed. What an alarming thought! It wasn't until a very good friend of mine looked at me and said, "Naomi, drink water and lots of it, now". I did and I instantly felt calmer. He then suggested that I replenish my body with highly advanced vitamins and mineral supplements which he supplied to me. Within a week, my skin cleared up, my hair and eyelashes stopped breaking and most importantly, my perception of life returned to my usual optimistic and proactive state. This allowed my breathing to become deeper and slower, resulting in my cortisol levels going down and my ever so important DHEA (the anti-ageing hormone) to rise, thus regenerating highly optimised younger cell production rather than the degenerate ones I was obviously producing. The unexpected surprise was that I even lost weight, 8 kg to be precise. Nowadays, when I walk down the road, walk in to shops or see people who I haven't seen for ages, they say I look as though I am in my early twenties and that I look great – well guess what? That is exactly how I feel!

It doesn't surprise me that many people spend thousands of pounds on mind set and inspirational workshops to achieve a new and better perspective on life. I too have conducted such important and life-changing workshops. However, I am a firm believer of the balance and connection of the Triad – BODY, MIND and SPIRIT. To achieve and enjoy any kind of enlightenment and abundance, one must focus on getting the body to resonate to its optimum capacity through good nutrition and lifestyle. That way, the frequency that one will give off will be highly magnetic. The highly intelligent information that will be emanating from the physical body will be more readily accessible, thus giving your perception of life a different perspective. Your choices and decisions will be sharper and clearer, so too will your focus, imagination and visualisations. Your overview of the world will come to the fore and your purpose will be revealed. This is the power of the foundation of self. Harness yours and the world will be nestled in the palm of your hands.

You see our body is definitely our temples, the place that holds the secret to who we really are. Each and every one of us chooses to reside in our particular bodies, so honour yours and the link between wellness, wealth and abundance will reveal itself to you.

## The Brain

The human brain weighs only three pounds but is estimated to have about 100 billion cells. Can you imagine - each one of those cells carries specific bits of information that can create your ideal future? It is hard to get a grip on a number that large (or connections that small) but the brain is the hardware workhouse of all the information that is stored in our energy fields. Under your instructions it will filter, distort and create any illusion that you care to programme it with. The two sides of the brain have distinct and separate functions which create the reality we see, hear, feel, taste and touch with our bodies. The left side of the brain is responsible for logic, writing, reasoning, number skills, speech, science, language, present and past and is detail orientated. The right side of the brain is responsible for creativity, imagination, music, three dimensional forms, feelings, the big picture, present and future possibilities and spatial perception. The right side of the brain will take all the visual inputs that you have ever had and put it together in a form. The left side of the brain will analyse that form and put a name to it. The most fascinating part about the brain is that it has access to every single piece of information that you were exposed to since birth via the subconscious and conscious mind. It is the machinery that makes sense of all this information and gives you solutions to any amount of problems or challenges you think you have.

Picture this: you have a challenge that you need to solve, so you engage the right side of your brain to look at the problem visually. At the same time, you instruct your left brain to find a solution and you are now using language and asking powerful question to which your brain computes answers. Your brain will go in to hyper drive to throw up infinite possible solutions to match the pictures you are visualising. If you stay quiet for a moment and allow the brain to carry out your instructions, the right brain and the left brain will work together to come up with the most suitable solution according to your belief systems and your values. You will suddenly get to a point where you feel tingly anticipation, indicating that you have nearly cracked it and thus comes your 'AHA' moment.

You see, the brain needs instructions to create the path to your destination. If you tell it that you are poor it will give you every single reason for you to justify your instructions. The brain always makes you right. Similarly, if you tell your brain you have created a school this year, it will find everything in its system to bring forth that reality because you are right. To work your brain so that it does what you instruct it to do quickly, it is important to create pathways of information that it can readily recognise. Every single one of those 100 billion cells has a special piece of information that you gave it. The more you do it, the more the cells cluster together to create a neural network of cells that then make your actions a habit. Give your brain information of good habits in wealth, health and relationships, and it will recognise those habits and respond by relaying the information to your body, your hormones and ultimately to your energy field.

## The Conscious Mind

One day, I asked my children a question: what is the difference between the brain and the mind? My son stuck his hand up in the air and said, "The brain is like a box and the mind is like the information inside the box". My daughter then added, "But the information doesn't have to stay in the box because it is energy and it can move wherever it likes." And finally my younger son said, "So that means the mind can be anywhere." Beautiful explanation.

We know that the world is a huge web of energy configured into different pockets of informational frequencies. We cannot see this as the bigger picture for several reasons. Firstly, the energy is vibrating far too fast for our eyes to pick up and secondly, we haven't trained our brains to pick up and understand such high frequencies without deleting the experience. This means that the human senses can only pick up certain bits of information which are chunked together to create form and matter. If our perceptions were trained to see higher frequencies we would all be able to observe and perceive the energy fields that surround us and that of others. You will also be able to see that we are all part of the same energy field and we all vibrate constantly at differing rates.

At any given moment, your energy field will come into contact with and affect everyone else's energy field and each of us will respond in some way to that experience. These pieces of information that we pick up every second of our existence form our emotional and mental makeup of what we call reality, which we experience through our senses. It is highly common to pick up feelings, emotions and thoughts that are not yours, but which you interpret and give meaning to thus creating them as yours. This just confirms the fact that we are a huge melting pot of ideas and emotions that we globally and communally share. This is the reason that sometimes in our lives we feel intrinsically connected and at one with the world – you literally are.

If we can perceive this every now and again, what is stopping us from perceiving it on a daily basis? The problem lies with the filter of our conscious mind. However, in order to get on with our three dimensional lives, our conscious mind filters out all the information that we feel is not self serving. We are constantly deleting and distorting reality in order to make sense of our world and match it to our belief systems. It is also exacerbated by the conditions and paradigm in which we have grown up. In a way, our conscious mind is there to protect us from information overload. However, it is possible to increase the amount of information we perceive in order to come closer to the full picture of what reality really is.

Quantum science is a wonderful thing, isn't it? But if it is dressed in scientific jargon it is quite mind-boggling when one is trying to understand what it all means to us today.

Well, think of it this way. We now understand that we are basically fields of energy, from a field that infinitely emanates around us right down to our physical cells and atoms and electrons – which are such high frequency we can hardly detect they are there. Our five senses fool us into thinking that we are fairly solid and have definition of form. Indeed it looks and feels that way when we see it from the human perspective but that is partly due to the types of conditioning or rather the current paradigm in which we live and partly due to the very real notion of the density of the physical body itself to allow for such thinking. We all see it this way because our five senses are vibrating at a certain frequency. This specific type of frequency (in accordance with our current paradigm) is only able to pick up a certain type of frequency which we can convert into form and meaning. Our five senses also confuse us and allow us to believe that what we see around us has form and structure that is fixed and stable. In fact, all that we see is an illusion of the senses. Change your personal paradigm; raise your energy frequency and right before your eyes the world changes like you've always dreamt. The basis of creation is to understand the substances in which one is to work.

Just think, if we were schooled into having a more accurate belief system of self, in that we possess an energy field which is probably more important than our physical bodies, we would start believing and then knowing that we have a powerful energy anatomy. That very belief system would automatically relay the information to our physical senses and allow us to perceive more information in order for us to actually see the energetic body with our physical eyes. The vibratory frequency of the receptors of our eyes would actually rise to match the information of our belief system and thought processes. This means that consciously, our minds would send validation to our brains that high frequency information is possible to decipher and this in turn would create more neural networks that would give you more of the same.

It is exactly the reason why dogs can naturally hear higher frequency than we can. Their receptors in the inner ear vibrate at a higher frequency than ours. I am sure that the dog's parents didn't tell them to stop being so silly; of course they didn't hear that high pitched whistle!!

## The Subconscious Mind

We came into this world with the ability to adapt and survive. We have a purpose for doing this which is linked to our higher consciousness. Our ability to download vast amounts of information is paramount to our existence, as it facilitates our survival on earth, in whatever circumstances we find ourselves. If this is the case, then there is a purpose to this particular type of ability. Our downloading takes place in our subconscious mind, and our subconscious mind is located within the very energy frequencies within our emotions and thoughts to the effervescent fields that are emitted from our physical bodies.

The subconscious mind processes twenty million environmental stimuli per second, and most of the time we are not even aware of the copious amounts of rich information that we have already downloaded. On the other hand, the conscious mind only process forty environmental stimuli in that same second.

In other words, when we were children, we had our realities energetically shaped for us in order to prepare us for the conformity of the environment in which we live. Before the age of six, we diligently picked up the programming of how to act and feel, what beliefs to believe in, what's right and wrong and so on. Like sponges, we absorbed it all. Whether you are aware of it or not, every single thing you experienced- good and bad- is logged and wired into your subconscious, ready to act out when necessary. This was not a bad thing because it allowed us to learn essential and relevant information on how to live on this earth, especially in the environment in which we find ourselves living.

Scientific research suggests that our subconscious mind is so vast that it can take over your conscious reasoning in a heartbeat. So maybe the key is to understand the programming of the subconscious mind in order to upgrade our conscious living. This of course means that the greatest opportunities we have on the earth right now to change our paradigms of self lie with children, as subconscious programming starts even before birth.

## The Spirit

In the domain of quantum physics, we would see that everything we think of as being solid in the physical world is actually flickering in and out in an infinite void at the speed of light. Even though our dulled five senses perceive things as solid, we are all in fact flickering in and out of existence all the time. Don't forget, everything has a frequency of vibration, so it is dynamic. We expand and contract. Expand and contract, constantly. This is the nature of anything that oscillates at a certain frequency.

When we talk about contraction of our selves and matter, we understand that we pull things into form by the nature of our thought process. What happens when we exhale and expand, and everything is seemingly out of form and whirls in dizzying speeds, way out to infinity for there are no boundaries? Where does our physical body go when we expand, and where do we go if we are not our physical bodies?

Our human bodies oscillate up and down at a rate of about 7 hertz per second. This rate of frequency is far too fast and minuscule for us to register or to be aware of within our own bodies because of the lower and slower vibrations of our five physical senses. The late twentieth century inventor Itzahak Bentov recognised that these vibrations or oscillations posses the same characteristics as the motion of a pendulum. In fact the nature of energy moves in the way a pendulum does, i.e., it pulsates concentrically, moves back and forth, travels in an orbit or turns about itself, thus the basic movement is back and forth, back and forth. Therefore, if everything in the Universe is made up of pure energy, then it moves in the same ways as a pendulum does, back and forth, back and forth. There is a secret and the secret is this: hidden within the movement of the pendulum is an amazing feature that not very many people save the mathematicians know about…

Pendulums have mystifying, mind-boggling feature at their point of stillness, as does anything that is at absolute rest. A pendulum swings back and then has to travel forth in order for it to comply with the rules of its motion. Before the pendulum swings back again it has to stop. Doesn't it? If it didn't, it would just keep going and that would go against the laws of physical nature. But it doesn't just stop! Just before the very point at which the pendulum starts on its return trip, it crosses a zero point, where 'all bets are off regarding the causal relationship between time and space'. At those two still points, (one on the back swing and one on the forth swing), the pendulum becomes for a very miniscule period of time nonmaterial and expands into space at infinite velocity. This means it disappears. Thanks to relative theory, this is a mathematical certainty and what this means for us is startling.

Our bodies are exactly like that pendulum. It oscillates at a rate of about 7-8 cycles (hertz) per second and therefore reaches a state of rest at about 14 times a second. That means that at least 14 times per second, we are expanding at a very high speed through subjective time into objective space. In no time at all, we come back again. But in that no time, that still time, we have been out in to other dimensions and realities, dispensing and collecting immense amounts of information. Each and every time we expand, we go back home. We experience the nature of our true essence, our true power, our true magnificence. We bring back wholesomeness, balance and love. We bring back information which results in to immense creations like electricity, telecommunications, the micro chip, etc. We are in our essence like an evolving software programme.

Why don't we know this? Our physical five senses are dull aren't they? So why don't we try to use our far more powerful and more accurate energetic senses? All one needs to do is focus on them. That is why in our three dimensional world we get inspirational Eureka! moments, and powerful insights. Some of us are more sensitive to the 'downloading' moments than others. However, we all have experienced synchronicities disguised as coincidences and that is because when we intend something, we literally put it out there. Time and space do not exist out there in the non local realm and our answer comes back immediately through various channels, as others pick up our messages and deliver our answers through synchronicity. It is part of the synchronized events that the late physicist David Bohm describes as the implicate order, which in fact is what we experience as the omnipresence of all that is and thus the universe. You may if you wish put a name to that omnipotent presence. Many people do; it is what you feel comfortable with.

This explains why a great idea can pop up all over the world at exactly the same time. We are all communicating at a much higher, global quantum level than we realise.

## Exploring Non Local Space

Our quantum scientists call the source The Non Local Domain, which is just a fancy term for the immense intelligence that co-ordinates and organizes the energy fields in which all things are enfolded. It encapsulates the infinite of the all, which is mirrored in the small- exactly like a hologram. There is no location or locality that one could pinpoint, for the very nature of consciousness itself is an expanding field of creative thought, non creative thought, creative non thought and non creative non thought. Its motion is inside out and back in again, contracting and expanding just like we do – funny that, isn't it?

This non local intelligence can cause multiple effects simultaneously in various locations. Due to the very nature of the intelligence, indirect cause and effect takes on a higher prevalence, orchestrating high degrees of instantaneous motions of creation, all at the same time in trillions of different physical locations. The non local domain responds to degrees of consistent and non consistent thought from locations all over its domain. It absorbs these pieces of information, contracts them and as it exhales, it instantly displays a response in the most exquisite of patterns. These patterns are of a divine nature and can never be faulty, as there are no stray strands of thought to be faulty with. Thought and higher forms of creation come from the all and manifests itself in the small.

This then is the source of the synchronicities that are so important to the creation of our destinies, here on earth and beyond. When one is able to keep ones attention and awareness at this level of self, and one learns to create with the essence of heart and self, you begin to understand that the world and more are literally at your beck and call. You will fulfil your every desire and create miracles because you are a complete embodiment and reflection of the universe itself – you are just displayed in a different frequency format. You will do yourself a great disservice if you think that this is a fancy notion that can be intellectualised. It is a state that can only be realised if it is experienced and owned. Many of us may not be able to feel the immensity of this information and that is totally okay. It is a matter of readiness that you and you alone will determine.

## The Pull of Readiness

We all have moments in our lives when we feel a pull of something we do not quite understand. It may be a rush of excitement or an intuition so strong that there must be something behind it, or even a strong feeling to change direction and paradigms of thought. What is that pull, why does it occur and what is its purpose?

That pull is a direct message from your higher self. It is in effect part of the blueprint of the story or journey that you are born with, which you are embarking on right now. For example, if you have gotten this far in the book, think about how timely any of the information that you have read resonated with you at this moment in your life. What was it that pulled you to read this book in the first place?

Which friend gave you this book and why? Or did you come across this book by pure 'coincidence'? Your energy field is absolutely full of information that pertains to your story, your journey and your mission. It constantly taps, pulls and tugs at your psyche for you to continue following your particular path. No path is right or wrong, because all paths are routes to higher learnings. These pulls occur in order to remind you of your purpose. You will feel and know these feelings from time to time because they sometimes come right out of the blue – with urgency! Or they will make you feel reflective, restless, uncomfortable, dreamy, anxious and many other types of feeling that states in bold letters TAKE ACTION.

Each time you have an irresistible urge to do something, pay attention and stay alert. Your higher purpose is prompting you. This emotional response came from the intention you personally designed for yourself, whether you know it or not. Your emotions stimulate a desire or a want and it deliberately makes you fidgety and restless, prompting a physical response which is a call to action. When you have activated this call to action, your mind will start overloading you with thousands of stimulating thought process, which will start organising themselves into a particular thought form. Visions of what to do, where to go, who to contact start to take form and at that moment in time, you are tapping into an incredible orchestration of creation, scanning the sea of infinite possibilities and creating pools of synchronicities. When you begin to focus and home in on the possibilities that resonate with you, start to focus on just one sequence of events. This event will surely become a probability. You are doing what scientists call 'collapsing the particle' – bringing one polarised set of events (within you) together with its entangled partner (what is perceived to be outside of you). Conceive it first; believe it, and then you will achieve it!

Every conceivable pathway to that call to action existed in front of you the moment your intention triggered you to an emotional response. Every conceivable solution to that emotional response was displayed before you and, unbeknown to you, in an array of perfect beauty – the dance of the matrix. At that precise moment, your high frequency thought process started to organise those fields of possibilities and very elegantly picked out ones that were matching its vibratory resonance. When a match became fixed, the effect came back as an idea, thus you collapsed the infinite array of ideas into one focused thought.

The thought has already matched the outcome, so your intentions are done! Whatever you desire you will manifest, providing you keep your emotional intensity lucid, strong and consistent. Pay attention to the synchronicities that surround you, use your intuition to navigate your physical senses.

One of the most exciting discoveries that has come out of science recently is that of entanglement. This basically means that we all in very intricate ways enmeshed with one another in an energetic fashion. You sitting there reading this book can affect another person's autonomic immune system-just by thinking about them!!! If at any moment you felt a resonate feeling whilst reading this book then you and I are not only entangled but I have certainly affected your nervous system – perhaps triggering off the process of you being upgraded; and, we haven't even met yet. How powerful is that? This has huge implications on how we communicate with each other and how we have been communicating with each other. We have been conditioned to believe that we communicate only through our five senses. In actuality, we are multilevel communicators, transmitting and receiving information simultaneously.

Our environment is directly shaped by our collective thoughts. We have created our planet in a true reflection of ourselves. Please remember that we are energetically entangled with all other organisms surrounding us. We in fact are in constant communication and entanglement with them as well. So whatever we do reflects back at us one hundred percent of the time. If you think about it, isn't that just a powerful tool, that we are able to highly communicate and affect every single thing on this planet instantly? The implications are enormous.

At this present time in current human history, we are strangling our physical creations. We are proving to ourselves that we are capable of destroying as well as creating. This, in the greater scheme of things, is fine; however humans have become imbalanced in the two different types of manifestations. The imbalance comes from a high degree of non self knowledge, which must be addressed if the current earth patterns are to regenerate and survive. If we persist in the imbalance of self, then the patterns of divine orchestration of which we are all part will continue until another creation of the planet is formed-which may or may not be self serving to the human being. Our spirit being of course will then choose again.

I do instinctively feel that it would be a shame for human beings to discard so much learning that we have accumulated over millennia. I know that a bigger and grander design of choice can be achieved, and with a conscious effort, it will be done easily and effortlessly and with grace. All it needs is a shift of perception. Are you ready for that shift?

# Chapter Five - The Infinite You

Okay, what do we know about the power of the universe?

We know implicitly that we are fields of energy.
We know for a fact that we are all essentially one body.
We know that these fields of energies are organised in a divine orchestration of synchronistic order.
We know that if we use the power of intent we can influence the synchronistic order.

When everything starts to come together and seemingly impossible events start to occur, we call this a state of flow. You are taken up by momentum and nothing seems to be able to stop that flow. This is due to clicking in to the implicate order. When you feel that state, lock into it because those are the synchronistic events that will shape your life and take you to higher planes of being. For at that moment you are riding the quantum leap that has perfectly balanced and reformed itself in to a new level of foundational self. This within itself creates new protocols, learnings and actions that are all part of your mission towards your perfect destiny.

Putting your attention on synchronicities and expecting them attracts more synchronicities. As one starts to unravel and reveal the meanings of these synchronicities, they then act as clues to the will of your higher self, providing the pathway to boundless possibilities.

## Living in Synchronicity

One of the most important things we need to do in order to realise our Life's purpose is to be very aware of the messages we send out through our energy systems. Very seldom do we check how we feel towards ourselves and our environment before we step out the door. Here are some steps that may be useful in order to get the best out of every day.

## Check Your Intentions Every Day

Remember, your energy field is the first point of contact with absolutely anything or anyone you encounter. What messages are you emitting?

Your energy field is capable of repelling and attracting anything, because it is a magnetic force. So be aware: if you are emitting a field that says, 'I am in a bad mood, stay away', that's exactly what you will encounter. Sadly, many people emit this type of energy field without even realising it because they have become accustomed to the emotional feeling it gives them and therefore it feels like it is a part of their natural characteristic make up.

What energy do you emit regularly? Are you happy with it? If not, change it. Run your energy to a higher vibration by breathing slowly and deeply for ten minutes and consciously change your state to one that makes you feel in control and powerful. Lock in to strong memories of a powerful self and use these memories to enhance and guide your state of emotions and mental change. Allow your body to resonate with coherence and feel the power of divine purpose coursing through your being. Look at yourself from the perspective of a spiritual being rather than that of a human being – you will be surprised how focused and comforted you will begin to feel. In time, you will not need the pseudo emotional armour that had become you, and whatever situation arose that instigated you to put that armour up in the first place will slowly dissipate to a more neutral energy.

## Letting Go

In order to allow yourself to grow your intuitive 'muscle' and recognise synchronised events, it is imperative to let go: to let go of your emotional barriers that are hindering the process of creation. Let go of the "what ifs" and the "yeah buts" and the limiting beliefs that will conditionally come up. Let go of the control you feel you want to have over the outcome of a desired event. Let go of the anxiety of wanting something so badly that you feel you may not get it.

Letting go is the process of trust and the process of relinquishing your need to be right and to be in control. Letting go means that you trust your powers of manifestation and you KNOW that they have already taken place, and all that is required of you is to observe. When one is in a state of detachment and balance, personal drama has less meaning because you trust that what you are creating is the actuality of self and not the thin reality of perceptual drama. This part of creation is probably the most important factor of manifesting your desired purpose. It is this process that will take time to master, as the layers of experiential conditioning from our current paradigm need to be peeled away and replaced with a new foundation of self. And as we know, to know thyself is to know the world.

## Ask Powerful Questions

Ask yourself and others powerful questions. Throw those questions out to the universe and then let go. Don't ponder about them, just trust that the answers are all around you. All you have to do is pick up the clues and be aware of the synchronistic events. A good time to throw up your questions is just before you meditate. If you are feeling stuck about which questions to ask, stand up. Walk around and ask the questions out loud to yourself. Listen to how you are phrasing them; rephrase them if you have to and listen to the answer that comes streaming through. This takes practice because do not forget that our bodies are made of dense material and it may take a bit of effort to pull the information through in terms of a thought process. Otherwise, if you are sensitive enough, you may be able to perceive the answers through many of our other communication ports, like intuition, dreams, feelings, sudden visions, etc.

## Be the Impeccable Warrior

Whilst you are developing your perceptual acuity, concentrate on heightening your five senses and become acutely aware of the things around you by being present and of the moment. Listen more to your surroundings. Focus on hearing something that is very faint like the flutter of butterfly wings or the purr of a cat sleeping that is across the road from you. Look at things from different angles using different focuses of your eyes. Notice the textures and the hues, the colours and the shapes. Eat your food more slowly and be aware that you are doing it. Consider whether the taste is delicious or mediocre and guess the ingredients if you didn't cook it. Become tactile like a child and awaken your sense of touch. Marvel at the different textures around you; the touch of the wind on your face, the way your skin feels when aroused, your heartbeat when you are deeply breathing, the feelings that surface when you touch the skin of a loved one. Use your sense of smell to discover pleasure or danger. For those of you who smoke, stop smoking for two weeks and notice the difference in smell and taste. Buy a new scent, sprinkle it on your bed and imagine the smell as though you were in another lifetime of secrets. You need to become the impeccable warrior, always poised to pick up the most important pieces of information that will create your destiny.

Keep a journal of all synchronicities and recognise the patterns. Do synchronicities occur more frequently at a certain time in your daily life, when perhaps when you are in a certain state? Do you trigger them by performing a certain act? Do you have a certain feeling of knowing that creates a miraculous event? These are things that we must all be focusing on daily. Know Thyself! When a synchronicity does arise, do not ignore it. Ask your self what's in the message. Does it have meaning? Follow it up consciously and listen intently. Develop a sense of super awareness.

## The State of Flow

You will find that after a while, you will be in the state of flow, where everything seems to come together beautifully and events and "good fortune" keep dropping into place. This is when all your work comes together in a beautiful motion of synchronicity: the power of creation. And although it seems that all these events are little miracles or perceived coincidental events that were happening outside of yourself, know that it is you that created those circumstances in the first place. Be very grounded when you click into this state as this sets the foundation for greater things.

## Gratitude

When parts of the puzzle to your destiny begin to take place, acknowledge each and every event with gratitude and give thanks to the universe for allowing you to realise the power within you. Gratitude is a curious thing because after all, to whom are you being grateful? Actually, it's you. You are the universe and the universe is you. Acknowledge this and gratitude takes on a whole new meaning.

## Keep Going

When you have reached your outcome or have achieved your destination, keep going. Create again. The ultimate purpose of life is to evolve to higher and higher states of creation to reach the definitive state of knowing our foundations of Self.

# Chapter Six - Moving Towards Evolvement

At the age of five, my mother used to make us three girls, her daughters, meditate. I had no idea what that meant or what it could do for us. All I knew is that I wanted to play outside our apartment like the other kids. Recently, I had a wonderful conversation with Dr. Dean Radin, the author of *Entangled Minds*, who told me that meditation actually changes the frontal cortex of the brain and allows one's awareness and perception to be altered. This means you are continuously preparing your brain for upgraded software.

As we know, we are not separate beings living in individual voids of experience. We are all so intimately connected that one cannot escape the fact that we affect each other and things with every breath we take. For millennia, we have been taught in schools that the beginnings of life as we know it began with a complex of gases, chemicals and energy that was not sustainable and therefore created the familiar event termed fondly, the Big Bang, and thus the creation of the universe as we know it. But do we really believe that the big bang was a random event created by chance as some scientists would have us believe?

The evolutionary chance theory is a worldwide scientific paradigm which we take for granted because scientists are seemingly one hundred percent sure of its validity. However, recent systematic and vigorous research proves that the chance theory is not possible and could not be possible due to one single flaw.

Hmm, what is that flaw?

Conventional science purports that the world was subject to random events that occurred by chance. Through those events, we are taught that self organising simple life began to flourish through trial and error and through the survival of the fittest theory; so anything that has become organised and intelligent has done so through learning and progressing. Anything that is out of the ordinary or that does not fit into the tightly banded chance theory is labelled an anomaly dismissed as a freak occurrence - again produced by chance. According to modern day science, these anomalies have no significance in the grand scheme of things because they fall outside of the mainstream paradigm of what we already know in science!

Let's take a closer look? Dr Gary Schwartz, the author of *The G.O.D Experiments* posed a very important question. Is it possible that this world was created by chance?

If you think about it, chance means that it just happened by accident, that is, it was not meant to happen and it was not planned to happen, in fact, something happened by mistake and it was a chance occurrence. If we take this notion and accept what the mainstream scientists tell us: that evolution just happened by chance and therefore by the process of trial and error and the survival of the fittest theory, mashed together with mutations and aberrations, then we are all just fancy mistakes. Do you feel like one?

We by chance happen to look like this and evolve like this and think like this until we got to the point were we happen, by chance to start thinking about a greater collective of higher intelligence - all by chance. Could it be possible that DNA was created by chance, therefore the computer chip was created by chance; skyscrapers and mobile phones were created by chance? And following on with this line of thinking, rockets that orbit the globe, telecommunications, high spectrum telescopes that can detect the age of a billion year old star was all perhaps by chance — a set of random equations that just happened to occur. Something is amiss. Something just doesn't feel right.

What frontier scientist now term the Zero Point Field is the closest we have gotten so far in understanding the intricacies of how systems, organisation, synchronicities, creations and feedback loops naturally occur in the global organism we call earth.

Going back to synchronicities, can we honestly say now that an out-of-the-blue, coincidental occurrence was a freak chance event? No, it was part of a design that You as creators created. And never before have these synchronicities held so much weight and importance as we move into the age of consciousness. Never before have we in the western world opened our minds to the possibility that there is a purpose to why we are living right here and right now. Never before have scientists so clearly and boldly kicked open the door to the evidence-based facts that are now starting to create a belief system so strong that it will shift our current paradigm.

Today you and I are in the midst of a tremendous change, and the best part of it is we are and can be conscious of that change. To move towards conscious evolvement is to remove yourself from the everyday drama and take a good bird's eye view of the wider universal picture. It takes imagination, feedback and consistent repetition to make any worthwhile change, and the biggest of these three in which we all must engage is imagination. As Einstein says, "Imagination is more important than knowledge."

## Way Past Time

"The distinction between past, present and future is only a stubbornly persistent illusion."

Albert Einstein

So it's time. In fact it was pointed out to me that it is way past time. So how do we understand and feel our grandest selves? How do we understand what our full potential actually looks like and then begin to live it? How do we upgrade ourselves in order to upgrade the world? The answer is so simple it may surprise you.

According to scientific research, our consciousness survives us after death. As I stated at the beginning of the book, I myself have gone through a Life Between Lives therapy with Andy Tomlinson, and the information that he drew from me was not only mind blowing for me but it warranted me being written into two of his books.

Life between lives is a state of consciousness that a trained hypnotherapist can elicit from you. Whilst under hypnosis, you are able to tap into information (that you already know but have perhaps forgotten) about what you were doing the moment you died in your past life to the moment you reincarnated into you current life! Mind blowing, right?

Because you are made of photons, the minute energetic particles that make up the appearance of matter of your body are by nature flicking in and out constantly, due to the fact that photons are weightless and have no mass. This means that you are constantly flicking in and out of universal information and the eternal now. No past, no future, just the now.

The source of information that is available to us every second we breathe is astounding, and the greatest thing about this awareness of knowledge is that we have the capacity to tap in to it in our everyday state of awareness. It is this knowledge of awareness that makes us move towards evolvement, and in that moment, awareness is what makes us so powerful. Dr. Gary Schwartz, whom I mentioned earlier, also wrote the groundbreaking book, *The Afterlife Experiments*. He created definitive experiments showing without a shadow of a doubt that our consciousness survives us after death. Therefore, we can easily sum up that the consciousness of others that have passed before us have already consciously survived their death and still exist energetically, and we have access to their information. What does this mean to you? This gives us the incentive, the drive and the encouragement even in our darkest hours, to be comforted in out times of need. You see, I believe that this life here on earth is an experiential one; we are here to experience our chosen lives, good and bad. Therefore our ability to detach ourselves from the physical and emotional drama we create is in our power and always has been. This life is not the be all and end all of existence. There is something far greater, and sublime, and intrinsically beautiful, and huge, and extremely complex that we all already know so well. I believe we are here to experience life on earth, and our task is to remember from whence we came and bring it in to manifested being.

## Manifesting Our Grandest Selves

As a wealth creator, I absolutely love what I do. My purpose in life is to raise the consciousness of humanity in order to affect global peace. I am passionate about sharing knowledge, especially with our younger generation, to transform the way they think about themselves in this world, thus allowing them the opportunity to make better and different choices than their predecessors. I have realised that we do not have to wait to make our millions to create real change in life. We have the capacity to do what we love and create wealth beyond our dreams with the knowledge we already posses. Our imagination is the key to setting us free. In truth, it is what we are here to do – to make manifest our grandest selves.

In my workshop, The Human Upgrade, we take our delegates through a process of knowing what a possible future could be for them through our given gift of precognition. Inevitably, when we go through this type of process and we take it to a global level it is startling to see that everyone sees the same thing. So on page 125 I am going to take you through one of the processes that takes you to a global vision. Let's see what you come up with.

This exercise came about because I couldn't get clear on the reasons why I was doing my workshops. I kept asking myself what was the outcome. What was I reaching for? What did that end result look like, and would I be satisfied with that vision? You see, I believe that we get confused and disoriented when we state things like, 'I want to get there. To that place of abundance'. That's great that you want to get 'there' but where is there? And what does it look like? What do you think it feels like? Are you clear on the final visions of the outcome? Can you see it in minute detail?

At the end of 2007 I saw an article in one of the national newspapers that headlined Sierra Leone as the poorest and the most unliveable country in the whole world. It was still in the dark ages and had amenities that would even shame those folks who lived 2000 years ago! Here I was, a wealth creator in a wealthy country talking about personal transformation, when in some areas of that country, their wealth creation stopped at the garbage and refuse that was lying in the corner of their no-electricity, rat infested, disease-festered shack that was so hot and putrid that it was difficult to breathe. In the picture in the newspaper, was a beautiful young girl who had every right to live a regular life that is owed to every child, but there she was holding her newly born baby, who was oblivious to the conditions that she was born into. According to the United Nations Human Index, Sierra Leone is (at the time of writing) 177th out of 177 countries in terms of wealth in GDP terms. I was truly horrified. I had heard of so many horrific human suffering stories over my young years that I had become almost anaesthetised until I read this story. Why did I cry so? What was in the story that made my heart open and my body shake with unadulterated compassion? What was pulling me? Yes, I recognised the pull of readiness, but what form would it take? I possessed all the answers and I understood all of them. By revealing my answers to you, I trust you will find an equally compelling story in your life that is similar to my own in terms of the resonance it gives you. The answers that I reveal will be the same answers that will apply to you. Trust me, we are truly one.

So, what was it that was affecting me so much? Fact No.1: I am a child of Sierra Leone. That child on the front of the newspaper could have been me, had my mother not had the foresight to follow her dreams and make a better life for herself. Fact No.2: Although Sierra Leone is the poorest country in the world, it has according to economists, the potential to be the richest country in Africa because of its rich soil and its abundance of minerals! (In fact it used to be the richest in its heyday). The richest in Africa! Fact No.3: The war that devastated Sierra Leone was due to diamonds; blood diamonds. I realised that if I am wealth, and I have the same blood as these Africans, then I am truly one of the diamonds that came from this country, therefore they too are wealth – and the majority of them just don't know it. The compassion I felt made me understand that I am truly entangled with them and because I am connected to the world they feel they cannot reach, I have the opportunity to show them a newer version of the world. Fact No. 4: The 'pull' was my life mission tapping at my consciousness, creating instant focus. I knew without a shadow of a doubt that all of my workshops whether they were for youth, adults or corporate institutions, all led the way to creating something better for children all over the world who are struggling for their basic right to live. I suddenly realised that my purpose was to lead the way to create powerful leaders of the next generation and it began in Sierra Leone and would soon spread all over the world.

That evening I rang my business partner and told him about the article. I cried again and I told him that I knew what the workshops were all about, why I created them and the purpose of them. But there was just one piece of the puzzle that hadn't been revealed to me yet – but that was to come sooner than I expected.

A week later, my business partner came over to discuss the newspaper article. And we put ourselves through a powerful process. I knew that time didn't exist, so I posed a question to him, "We know that time doesn't exist, right?

So that means the future is sitting with us now and we have the ability to perceive that future. What would happen if we looked at the future right now and saw the outcome of our beliefs? What if we dared to be bold enough to state this as our reality and make it happen? What if?"

He said, "Let's do it". So we did. He first asked me what the world looked like in the year 5007. Wow, we were at a time that was 3000 years from now. I was in the hotseat. I stood up and centred my self. I did a breathing exercise that clears my head and readies me to stand on my foundation of self. I started walking and feeling the time of 5007. My body shivered in anticipation and I knew I was there. I started talking. And guess what I saw? I saw schools. And they were Schools of High Conscious Awareness (SOHCA Schools). They were everywhere, in every country, city, and village. They were the norm and they were common. They were run by large community groups that were dedicated to child development to the highest degree. They all had huge global connections and they were awesome. They had technology that I couldn't see because at this point they were unimaginable to me. The children playing in the fields and classrooms were participating in activities that were truly foreign to my mind but they were happy, healthy and highly consciously aware. It was as though they sensed me watching. And they smiled. My heart leapt but it wasn't at this point that I cried. More was to come.

My business partner told me that it was the year 3007. My vision shifted and I saw a bit of turbulence. Children were powerfully demanding the right to be free to learn. The schools were there but not as abundantly prevalent as in the previous vision. I was awed by so much change in the world as there was huge progress but a lot of work was still to be done.

I was then asked to enter the period of 2507- 500 years in front of me. Again, there were even fewer schools but they had prestige and were favoured by parents wanting to put their children through a holistic type of education. They were seen as elite schools for the poor, but at the same time, the children who attended these schools were seen as being of a higher conscious nature. They thought differently, had greater facets of ideas; imagination and technology were the foundations of the school, and they became great global leaders. Times were finally changing.

It was now 2157- 150 years in front of me. This is the point at which I cried. I saw my direct descendants leading the SOHCA schools to higher degrees of Excellency. I heard my great, great grandchildren laugh and I intuited that they said, 'You were always on the right path'. I cried so hard I couldn't go on but I had to see the beginning.

I was brought to 2057. Tears and snot were running down my face but I so didn't care because I knew that I was about to arrive. There are a few hundred Schools of High Conscious Awareness on this planet. And they are very special. I knew my company was the instigator of these schools. I am still young but my body is getting tired. I know that soon I will finally die with a huge smile and a sigh. I did it. I initiated the creation of the 5000 year reality in this life time.

I was brought to the present day. I fell to my knees. I knew what was to be done. I was to create the opportunity for people who resonate with the idea of the school to join me to create the very first SOHCA School situated in Matamp, Sierra Leone. It was to be introduced in January 2008, and it was. The first phase of the building of the foundations takes place in November 2008. At this point I knew I had arrived and all the rest is just detail.

It has been exactly a year since that powerful vision and I can proudly say that the foundations of the very first SOHCA School have been laid and the building is now being erected. In fact, if you bought this book, you contributed to the build as well – so from the bottom of my heart I thank you.

Going through these powerful processes released me from the uncertainty of my future and the confusion about what others think I should be doing with what I have. I know what I have to do. I have seen it. The power of self realisation is liberating and enlightening. Nothing is clearer than my purpose and mission in life and this is the sole purpose of this book; to awaken your vision of your purpose and mission. Your personal transformation globally affects our world - yours and mine. Very soon I will take you through the same process that I described earlier. Once you get the hang of experiencing how powerful your visions really, are you will start to gain emotional clarity. It will be at this moment that you start jumping into the pool of quantum manifestation as your energetic signature code will transmit way out to the universe.

Are you ready to start tapping in to your higher self? Okay, let's do it. Before we begin, it is important to have the desire, the knowing and confidence that what you see, feel and perceive is a reality, but not as you know it. You can do this on your own or better still, you can ask a friend or someone who is just as excited about this process to lead you through it. You can then do the same for them. It is also important to move or walk around, as this stimulates the emotional response you will receive when entering the global future.

Start by projecting your awareness to a place that is 500 years in front of you and then follow the procedure below.

## Discovering your world View

500 Years from Now

250 Years from Now

150 Years from Now




100 Years from Now




50 Years from Now




What did you do today that reverberated in your 500 year vision?

Now that you have a vision of what your purpose and mission is all about, write it down and continually redefine it until it sits comfortably with you. Take this vision and sit quietly by yourself and ask: what do you need to do? Who do you need to see? What do you need to feel to just begin this project? Take small steps. Later, perhaps tomorrow, divide your vision into small doable chunks and ask your subconscious to bring you the people, events and tools to start manifesting your vision. Most importantly, see the picture of each chunk happening in your head. What are you wearing? What are you saying to whom? Where are you?

The answer that I had all along was the yearning desire to create compassionate advancement of all species on this earth so we can all live in trust, love, harmony and peace. We need a radical change in our institutions and I know we all feel it. The question that is always asked is what can I do about it? My answer is simple – upgrade yourself. After all, isn't it acceptable to throw away technology, toys and tools when they are outdated only to buy a new innovative upgrade? It's time to put that type of attention upon ourselves and throw away institutions, beliefs and values that no longer serve humanity.

## Upgrades - Presentiment

Throughout the last decade, huge advancements in our human potential have been illuminated to us especially in books like *The Entangled Mind* by Dr. Dean Radin, in which he talks of presentiment. This skill that we posses, albeit unconsciously, is one of the keys to recognising future events that are actually happening now!

Presentiment is the ability to perceive an emotional response to a future event. According to Dean Radin, we are 'constantly and unconsciously scanning our future and preparing to respond to it'. He also stated that "Presentiment experiments provide a new form of evidence suggesting that we can unconsciously perceive our future". What would happen if we pushed the boundaries and consciously perceived our future? It only takes you to try it and prove it to yourself.

If you think about it, all of this suggests that our understanding of time is seriously flawed and incomplete. Studies on presentiment show that some aspect of our minds can perceive the future, and that means that you can perceive it too!

A few years back when my twins were four years old, we took them on holiday to visit their relatives in Calabria Italy. I remember sitting in the front room and talking to some of the adults when suddenly my awareness of the children playing outside was heightened. It felt like my whole body expanded. My concentration on what the previous conversation was with the adults shifted as it moved to how my body and especially how my feelings felt at that moment in time. I suddenly felt my body brace itself, as though I was about to get hurt. How curious. This made my senses even more acute and I listened out for the noises of my children playing outside. Everything sounded normal, so I started to relax. Five minutes had gone by and suddenly I heard a massive smash, and two seconds later I heard my son screaming out "Mama!". I rushed outside as he rushed in and saw a massive, big, angry bump starting to swell on the front of his forehead where he had just collided with the edge of a wall. It was at that moment that I realised that I had felt this accident only minutes before. Could I have prevented this accident by directly going outside the moment I sensed something was wrong? Would I have changed the course of a future event? You bet. What had stopped me was a mixture of an overlay of rational thinking, failing to connect the heightened awareness of the noise of the children playing with the bracing effect moments afterwards. This directly led to the uncertainty of my ability to perceive the future. However, as much as I can help it, that will never happen again.

The most powerful revelation that I discovered as to what empowers us is the experience of our innate abilities and the awareness of what had gone on. Being consciously aware of new ways of living upgrades our internal software and redefines the output of our experiences.

## Upgrades – Lucid Dreaming

In 2003, after I stopped working in television, I decided to become financially free. It wasn't necessarily because I wanted financial abundance, although of course I knew that was a major feature in my life, but more than anything else I just wanted my time back. I wanted to be free of any time constrictions that were not of my making. I wanted to start my businesses and raise my children to be phenomenal leaders of the next generation. I wanted my family to travel and become a force for good within the global community. I wanted to be known as a woman who made her mark on this earth. Yes, I was passionate about it. I had no idea how I was going to get to financial freedom and I had not a clue about what financial vehicle I was going to take.

As it so happened, one of the guys who lived at my home came into the kitchen, handed me a flyer and said, "Here, I think you'll be interested in this, it's one of those get rich quick schemes" – and then he half chuckled and half sneered at the flyer and walked away.

I picked it up and my eyes nearly fell out their sockets. There on the table in front of me was a flier that stated that one could become financially free through property education. I stared at it and my body resonated, vibrated did whatever it needed to do to tell me that I needed to go to the preview that they were advertising. I went and paid up the amount for the workshop, and believe me, that course of action was the beginning of my financial freedom. But it didn't stop there.

Two years later I was part of the Wealth Intelligence Academy, training to present one of their three day workshops. On one of these training days, I had to do a segment to a live audience. The night before, I couldn't sleep. I was in a strange hotel, in an unfamiliar bed and about to make my debut on the stage as a property education presenter. I still couldn't sleep and I felt like I was time-watching all night which made me feel very nervous about my performance the next day. I begged my body to relax and sleep but that night it was stubborn. It turned 6.30am and I could feel my eyes starting to get heavy. I begged my body to wake up at 7.30am as I didn't want to oversleep – what a mess!

I was terrified of not getting up on time but nevertheless I felt myself falling into a deep sleep. All of a sudden I felt like I was in a terrifying place and I commanded my consciousness to wake up immediately because I just didn't want to go through a nightmare. You know how it is when you make yourself wake up form a bad dream. So as I woke up I felt relieved but instantly recognised that I was actually in another dream! This really was a nightmare!

Orientating myself in the dream, I woke up to the most beautiful house I had ever seen. I walk in and gasped at the gorgeous, simple opulence. I noticed huge French windows that over looked the ocean and patio. I was absolutely astounded at the beauty of this house. Right in front of me I saw my husband, whom I didn't know in real life but I knew him as my husband in my dream. I asked him whose house this was and he said it was mine. I choked. For real? Anyway, to cut a long story short, I asked what time did I usually go to work and he said in five minutes. When I looked up at the clock it was 13.20 in the afternoon. I looked around, savouring the feeling of living in this fabulous house and made moves to leave at 13.25. When I really woke up in my reality I quickly looked over at the clock and saw the time reading 07.25. I gasped. Where was I? I must have been in a place that was approximately six hours ahead of me so that was somewhere east of where I was waking up on that day. Most importantly, I knew that what I experienced was a future probability that I could manifest as a future fact. How did I know? I recognised the feeling I had in my body. It was a sure knowingness, as though it was already happening. Throughout the whole weekend at that workshop, nothing could have pulled me down from that high feeling. I knew what my future house looked like, right down to the shine on the huge oak table!

Lucid dreaming is the phenomenon of being aware that you are asleep and interacting with your dreams.

Major dream research has been conducted throughout the last and current century indicating that lucid dreams, especially of the precognitive kind, are relevant and important phenomena in our lives.

Lucid Dreaming allows us to understand the unconscious mechanism of our traits and correct them if they are not desirable. It also allows us to understand the nature of time and how we interact with space/time.

## Upgrades: Precognition

Quantum theory indicates that there are no such things as separate parts in reality, but instead only intimately related phenomena so bound up with each other as to be inseparable.

Our ability to expand our personal awareness through time as well as space provides the strongest possible evidence for our timeless existence. We can learn to reside outside of time in a place free of depression about the past, fear about the future or anxiety about the present. This spacious state of timelessness manifests as the quiet mind. Our ability to move our awareness deliberately through time and space offers powerful, life changing experiences, demonstrating clearly that we are not merely bodies, but rather timeless awareness residing in a body.

Precognitive dreams are probably the most common psychic occurrence in the life of the average person. These dreams often give us a glimpse of events that we will experience the next day or in the near future. In fact, it has been proven that precognitive dreams may be caused by events that have already happened in the future. An example that is sometimes sited by the researchers is this: if you had a dream the night before that you saw an elephant pass by your window and the next day you woke up to find that a circus parade led by an elephant was passing down your street, that previous night's dream was caused by you seeing the elephant the next morning. A huge amount of data supports this phenomenon.

Precognitive dreams have an unusual preternatural clarity to them and they are mostly emotive in nature. Take 9/11. There were many reportings of people having strange, horrific dreams of planes crashing the night before that fatal day, which resulted in fewer people taking flights the next morning! How can we use this in our lives? Is it possible to change a future that we do not like due to precognitive information? Scientific research says yes.

My theory is, if we are getting information about what is actually happening in the probable future, then we have somehow aligned ourselves to that probable future, which is now more concrete as we move towards it. So what would happen if we were to realign ourselves with the most possible future instead and 'force the information' out there with a different energy alignment, different emotions, different thoughts, so we allow the probable future to send back signals that we are on the right path? The key is alignment and having that alignment embedded in our system.

And we don't have to dream to make it happen. If truth be known, we are dreaming all the time. Our greatest inventions come from us using our imaginations. And when we are in the state of imagining things, we are in the elements of dreaming. So let's think about this logically. If you are dreaming or imagining something that you want to make happen and you act upon it until it is manifest, did you not step in to the future and experience it in detail in your head first before you experienced it physically? Sure you did. That's what makes you so powerful – you are able to preview what you want in the future before you experience it. And if you experience 'your future' now, you create a resonant field of vibratory frequency around the emotional aspects of how you feel about that future, and because your field is magnetic you pull your future towards you because you and it are one. I call it the click and stick formula. It is that simple.

Understanding that you are already in your future is another paradigm shift we must make and this takes courage, as it breaks through thousands of years of conditioning about how we live in linear time.

# Timely Thoughts

My children believe that every day is today. This struck me as the natural state of the human beings. What would happen if we had no time construct, if past, present and future were blurred? Time in the real sense does not exist. We are so used to understanding time in chunks, due to the cycles that were observed from the beginning of time. The cycles of life gave early philosophers and observers the incentive to follow the rhythms of life mechanically using astronomy. We sense the passage of time in our personal experience and observe it in the world around us. We feel, think, and act in the flow of time.

Einstein said, "Space and time are modes by which we think, not conditions under which we live." The measurement of time is an ancient science, though many of its discoveries are relatively recent.

A few months ago, I had a tele-seminar conference with Dr. Dean Radin from the Boundary Institute. I told him about the process of using precognition and presentiment to tap in to our future lives, which of course is all happening now. He told me that in main, most people believe that the future is somewhere out there and that they are moving towards it. In actuality our consciousness is already out there, as it is part of the universe itself, which is omnipresent. So therefore we are connected to the future right now. Really understanding and feeling this type of information is truly a paradigm shift, and one we must make.

Knowing that I affect my 'future' reality injected a joy and a certain type of reverent playfulness into my life. I realised that I could home in on my future reality even more, so I decided to create The Future History Project, which is one of the most powerful tools I use to create my reality.

The Future History Project requires imagination and feelings. It engages both sides of the brain, the right side and the left side, which together compute huge amounts of information that when exacted correctly, throws up important insights and 'aha' moments. These insights are not just 'guesstimations' of information that your mind sloppily presents to you; these bits of information are the sum of everything you have experienced and have decided to experience in order to create the life that you already know that you are destined to live. This is perhaps why some of us feel like we haven't lived to our full potential because we have planned something in our between lives and our present conditionings have prevented us from reaching those heights of victory. The worst thing is that most of us don't even know it.

# The Future History Project

*Project Name:*

*State who you are and your purpose:*

# The Collapsed Future Layer Process

Take a 5 minute episode that you desire in the future and make it very specific. Write it down below.

Imagine you have no clothes on. Describe what your body looks like:

Now put clothes on your body. Describe precisely what your clothes look like:

Describe what your clothes feel like on your body:

Describe the precise actions of your body in this 5 minute episode:

Describe what you are feeling in this 5 minute episode:

Describe what you are thinking in this 5 minute episode:

Describe what you smell in this 5 minute episode:

Describe what you are seeing around you in this 5 minute episode:

Describe the taste in your mouth in this 5 minute episode:

Describe what you are hearing in this 5 minute episode:

Describe what you are intuiting in this 5 minute episode:

Describe what happened the next day:

After you have completed the layering process, it is very important to read over this document every single day for at least 21 days.

You can make this process even more powerful by recording it and listening to your future on CD or an ipod. By doing this you LOCK in the resonant information. You are then free to LISTEN to your vision, thus allowing the frequency of the information to deeply resonate on a biomolecular level. Your cells will absorb and remember this information and will transmit (broadcast) energy and information to the world. Your energy field will resonate, CLICK and STICK with like energy frequency and it will bring towards you that which you desire. Remember that your energy field is highly magnetic!

# Chapter Seven - Expansive Knowledge

It is because we live in a non local reality, which is to say that we can be affected by events that are distant from our ordinary awareness, that we are constantly absorbing, processing and being affected by information that we are not even remotely aware of. This motion drives experimental scientists crazy because it means that their laboratory experiments are subject to outside influences that may be beyond their control and knowledge. In fact, the data from precognitive research strongly suggests that an experiment could in principle be affected by a signal sent from the future.

Scientific data suggests that all of space/time is available to your consciousness – right where you are sitting, right now. You are in fact beyond the observer – you literally participate in the manifestation of the current world in which we live.

So how does consciousness access the non local space? Scientists believe, as do I, that it does so through the process of intentionality, which is fundamental to any goal oriented process, including retrieval of memory. In fact, the universality of non locality is simply there, existing as the fundamental nature of space and time. That is, it is a non physical thing but it is available and accessible at will. The makeup of this infinite non local space is most commonly described as the zero point field, the field, the matrix, the divine matrix and so on. Ultimately, this matrix, like a computer, holds all the information that there ever was and connects the information according to your intentions. Therefore your whole consciousness is the software, in modern technical speak.

Through an abundance of scientific research, it is clear that all of us have access to non local space. Without a doubt, people can learn to use their intuitive consciousness in a way that transcends conventional understanding of space and time to describe and experience places and events that are blocked from the ordinary perception. In other words, you can upgrade your software.

According to the great writer Aldous Huxley, the world is like a great thought rather than a great machine, and we can access the entire universe through our consciousness and our non local minds. So in fact we are of a dualistic nature - one that is local and material and one that is non local and non material. So what is our collective purpose? Is it not to continually upgrade ourselves and know ourselves as universal spirits and then help others to do likewise? We can only do this if we learn to upgrade ourselves first and then be the beacon of light, so others can follow.

## Knowing the Beginning

As was stated earlier in this book, one of the greatest gifts we can give ourselves is that of meditation.

Through meditation, one experiences an increasing unity of consciousness as one passes through the great chain of physical, biological, mental, spiritual, emotional and etheric levels of awareness. Through meditation, one experiences the insight that creates wholeness and coherence.

Separation is an illusion. And self realization means that one has the wisdom and knowing of who one is, and furthermore has embodied that wisdom. We often view awakening as a first step toward such realization. This can occur in a blink of an eye but often through the opening of one's heart through teachings and profound and oftentimes heartbreaking experiences.

These experiences serve as the catalyst for seeking new information and change. Knowing that we are conditioned to see things before we believe them, I found it very useful to show my clients what their energy fields looked like before I commenced with any bio energetic therapies. In this case, seeing is believing, and that starts the process of knowing the beginning - the beginning of you and your foundations of self. It is amazing how connective people become when they see their own fields staring at them from a big screen. For them it is proof that they weren't making all those symptoms up, for you can see the incoherencies in their energetic fields. The tool that I usually use for this purpose is Gas Discharge Visualisation.

We know that we are made up of energy and this energy has different frequencies. We also know in science that our psychic, emotional and mental fields can and do affect our physical bodies. Therefore, if we are harbouring thoughts or energies that do not serve us in these fields, they will be in incoherent or in disharmony with the natural state of our bodies. Usually they are not persistent and we are able to counteract them. But frequently, these 'negative' or non conducive energy fields linger and cause a whole lot of entropy of which we are not yet conscious. When we are not conscious of these fields, then we start to believe emotionally that our failings are our inherent nature and then we act accordingly to our 'pseudo nature'. Conditioning from our parents, families, schools and society can exacerbate the quality of our energy system and can prevent us from experiencing our grandest selves. So sometimes before we even begin to upgrade our software, it is important to go through a process of knowing, healing and self realisation.

## Taking a Moment

In our workshops, one of the most powerful ways we begin this process of knowing, healing and self realisation is through a process I call Moments of Self Recognition.

Enclosed with this book is a CD gift which I dedicate to you. If you do not have a physical copy, then you can download it at www.globalinfinity.co.uk.

Years ago, I went through a really dark period of my life. It was an extremely powerful and emotional period as I felt that I was totally alone in my journey of self discovery. I felt that no-one really understood what I was saying and furthermore, that they were not interested. I had three young children to look after, a company to run, a host of properties to manage and maintain, let alone my own, and a burning desire to lift myself to another level of being. On the outside it looked as though I had it all. But if truth was to be told, I felt like I was losing everything within and I just couldn't find my foundation of self. Things manifested abundantly on the outside but it did not mirror what I felt inside and I started to question who I was. What was I all about? And how did I fit in to this vast, beautiful world? The only place I could turn was inside and it hurt. I remember crumpling to the floor one afternoon, crying my eyes out and wishing that I was back at home. However home was not a location on earth; it was most definitely somewhere else and I couldn't find the vehicle to get there. As I sank deeper and deeper into what I wanted which was oblivion and stillness, I found myself writing a letter to myself in my head. I gently reminded myself that I didn't need outside validation. I was the valuator of self because I was one with the universe. All I needed was me, as I was the universe. If someone were to congratulate me it had to be me, for it is I who recognises my efforts. If I were to look for confirmation of the decisions I make, then it is I who should confirm my feelings of trust. If I were to look for love, then it is I who should love myself first before I sought to love anyone else. This process went on and on for a period of time of which I was not aware. In essence, I realised that unless I became whole within myself first in every aspect, then I would always see and experience a conflict within and outside of myself. I inwardly travelled to the child that I was and still am and recognised that the purest essence of me was in my innocence. I recognised that all the things I had done when I was much younger and all the things I had experienced that were out of the ordinary, were all truisms of self. I realised that if they were true of me, then they were true of us all as well. I also realised that the activities that I was passionate about when I was very young were indications of my purpose and mission in life. Those passions still exist today and they subconsciously guided me towards my grandest self. The two aspects of me, the adult and the child finally, became one and it was at that moment that I recognised who I was and what I wanted to give back to my world.

So with greatest love and respect, I recorded what I went through and I give it to you as a gift of love. Before listening to the CD, be sure to have 15 minutes of non interrupted time and space. Close your eyes when listening to the words and take yourself back to yourself as instructed. Physically, emotionally and mentally act out the instructions on the CD and honour and respect all emotions, feelings, thoughts and visions that may come up. Unify them all and become one. And remember, the universe is holding you softly in the palm of its hands for all times.

# After

The morning my friend called me a witch, I had woken up with my heart palpitating. I was disorientated and I still felt like I was in the dream that I had just woken up from. Try as I might, I could not shake off this strange feeling of unease. It was around 8:15am and I strolled into the kitchen, where my best friend was preparing to have breakfast. Two other students from our student accommodation walked into the kitchen and sat down. I was still disorientated when my friend asked me what was wrong. I told her that I had a dream that seemed really real and I couldn't shake off the feeling. I proceeded to tell them the dream and it went like this...

I walked into the kitchen and sat down with my three friends. Suddenly another student came crashing in. She threw her bag and keys on the white kitchen counter and started sobbing heavily. Immediately in my dream I said, "Jane, what's wrong?" Through her snotty nose and teary sobs she told us that her boyfriend had left her and that he had demanded the keys back to his apartment. The woman was distraught and it distressed me.

After I finished relaying the dream to my college mates, they all shrugged their shoulders and couldn't understand what my agitation was all about. It wasn't long before they saw things my way…

Exactly five minutes later, Jane comes crashing through the kitchen, throws her keys and bag on the counter and starts crying her eyes out. Immediately I said, "Jane, what's wrong?" The moment I said that, I felt I was in a déjà vu. I had just said those very words moments before. I stared at Jane. Within the next two minutes, Jane relayed her story nearly word for word as in my dream. My three friends were also looking at Jane as though she was some alien, but I realised it wasn't her they were baffled with; it was the bizarre moment of recognition that we shared at that moment. It was then that my friend turned to me and said, "Naomi, you're a witch!" All day I was in a daze, but now I know that for me, that statement my friend so graciously bestowed upon me was an indication that I was indeed in the process of being upgraded!

## Global Responsibility

It is time for us not only to take responsibility for ourselves but for the world. It is time to wake up and it is time to grow up. We have a glorious duty to perform and that is to bring forth our grandest selves into manifestation on this beautiful blue planet. The consequences of not taking that responsibility are unthinkable. Our connection to each other and the earth is undeniable. Wouldn't you want to keep the family around you safe, loved and progressive? Well now your family has just got bigger!

## SOHCA Schools

The SOHCA school programme is a continuous educational building programme dedicated to creating schools in developing countries. The sole purpose of the school is to produce high conscious leaders of the next generation until the vision outlined earlier in the book is complete. If you resonate with that vision and would like to join me in building these schools all over the world, then I would be immensely honoured and grateful. Synchronicity may have brought you to this exact point - who knows what you will unveil?

If you would like to join the SOHCA School Project and travel to Sierra Leone to physically contribute toward building the school, please contact Francine Beleyi on sylv122005@yahoo.fr . For more information about the Future History Project, GDV or The Human Upgrade workshops please email your enquiries to info@ globalinfinity.co.uk.

# Solving the Humpty Dumpty Syndrome

Humpty Dumpty sat on a wall
Humpty Dumpty had a huge fall, oh
dear!
All the king's horses and all the king's men
Hadn't a clue how to put Humpty togeth-
er again!

So…

Little Miss Muffet sat on her Tuffet,
Sobbing her heart away,
Along came a feeling
Which was full of creative meaning, and
she said,

"Sod it! I need an UPGRADE".

# About The Author

Naomi Sesay is one of the most exciting personal life evolvement speakers to come out of the UK. Her experience derives from the high pressure environment of television broadcast to the mind-boggling world of Quantum Physics.

Naomi has taken individuals and groups of people who were facing social, business, and economic challenges and turned their lives around with phenomenal success. She's also worked with schools, charities, Her Majesty's Prison Services and corporate entities to share her life changing tools.

Naomi is a serial entrepreneur and director of three companies, including Global Infinity, SOHCA (School of High Conscious Awareness) and the Billionaire Lady's Club. She is the creator of life transformational workshops including 'The Human Upgrade', 'Create Change' (an entrepreneurship program for economically challenged women) and 'Reality Check' (a youth programme), which are all paving the way to raising the consciousness of humanity. She attributes much of her business success to a new approach to social enterprise, which has led her to build a unique school in Sierra Leone – the poorest country in the world.

Lightning Source UK Ltd.
Milton Keynes UK
05 September 2009
143389UK00001B/7/P

9 781438 947495